Commendations

As it turns out, our age is not quite so *secular* as we thought. The purely pluralistic, live-and-let-live, totally tolerant society that promised to transcend religious conflict was always an illusion. The fool may be able to say in his heart that there is no Jehovah God, but he cannot, try as he might, quite extinguish the *sensus divinitatis*. Man's religious affections must be directed somewhere.

In this brisk, invigorating, highly readable book, Ascol and Longshore call on Christians to get *woke*, so to speak, to the present situation. That is, they diagnose what really ails our culture—the ascendency of a new religion that is, indeed, God-less but not deity-less; secular but not re-ligion-less. This new religion comes in many forms, but it is always and everywhere tyrannical. Its yoke is not easy, its burden heavy. Its god is the autonomous, ever-malleable self. Its sacrament is destructive, its liturgy gobbledygook, and its eschatology an unforgiving immanentization of the eschaton.

But the authors don't stop with a Sun Tzu diagnosis. A much-needed call to arms, a call to recovery of doctrine and practice, is issued. Evangelicals have been resting on their laurels—the vestiges of a bygone era—for so long that they have not yet realized that they have real competition on the block. They haven't noticed the insurgency that is captivating the hearts and minds of their sons and daughters. More dire still, they have forgotten how to put on the full armor of God and meet the enemy in the field head on. Ascol and Longshore are clear-eyed but confident in their assessment, hopeful in their plea, and determined in their charge. Do get this timely book.

Timon Cline
Writer at *Modern Reformation* and *Conciliar Post*, and
contributor to *By What Standard? God's World...God's Rules.*

I am thankful that for years Tom Ascol and Jared Longshore have been sounding the alarm of the dangers of social justice. It is as if the strong winds of social justice that have been blowing out of Europe have gathered into a massive hurricane over the Atlantic Ocean. The outer bands of this horrific storm have long ago made landfall here in North America—having already inflicted much damage to the American church.

Sadly, for many evangelical leaders, their alarm has fallen on deaf ears. Not willing to be perceived as offensive or divisive, many Christians have chosen to remain silent or, even worse, embrace social justice. The evangelical church is starting to be torn asunder. But the real damage of social justice is still pending. When the eye of the hurricane arrives (if it hasn't already arrived in the year 2020), social justice will wreak utter havoc on those who remain unprepared. If the church does nothing, if the church doesn't prepare and board up its windows and doors by equipping the saints to hold fast, I am not sure what will remain standing.

With such a devastating tempest approaching, I want to stand alongside Tom and Jared and encourage everyone to read this book. My plea is for pastors and Christians to heed this clear alarm and secure multiple copies of this book to share with everyone they know. Tom and Jared rightly describe social justice as "the new religion of secularism." They explain that it has a false gospel, a false law, a false priesthood, a false spirit, and a false god ("worshiping creation rather than the Creator"). But, unlike Christianity, this new religion prohibits the liberty of conscience and the freedom of speech. It has no room for disagreement. And even more dangerous, this new religion seeks, through political activism, to wield the power of the sword so it can censor those who do not bow the knee to their unjust view of justice.

How is the church to endure the furious winds of social justice? The remedy, according to Tom and Jared, is found in affirming the biblical distinction between law and gospel, educating our children, affirming our commitment to the local church, and reminding our civil authorities that Christ will justly judge them by His law. There is much work to be done in the days ahead of us. Thus, I hope you will join me in trying to get this book into as many hands as possible. This is an excellent book that is much needed.

Jeffrey D. Johnson
Pastor of Grace Bible Church and
President of Grace Bible Theological Seminary, Conway, AR

In 2020, a very real virus was used as the rationale for restricting civil and religious liberties and justifying government intrusion into the *when*, *where*, and *how* of corporate worship services, revealing that Christians in the United States of America face the same problem as many pastors. Desiring to be liked, we grow lax in speaking words that would bring conviction concerning the sins in the room. A misguided attempt to maintain public witness has become a means whereby we affirm popular pagan ideologies. Unquestioned subservience to secular society is seen as a way to sustain our social capital. Whereas Christians of yesteryear did not fear death, preached the hard truths of Scripture regardless of the results, and either fled from or fought against tyranny, today our attitudes and actions toward the aforementioned ideals are virtually indistinguishable from those of the world. The colonists of America look petty in light of what we have endured in 2020. The convictions for which Christians were once willing to die are seen as unnecessarily divisive today. What was once valued as virtuous is now considered selfish and evil.

But the recognition of God-given rights by government authorities is not only good for you and me; it is good for the spread of the gospel, human flourishing, and the glory of God. If our government was made for a religious and moral people then we shirk our duties when we keep our Christian faith from the public square. Our countrymen are some of our nearest neighbors. We cannot in good conscience sit idly by and kowtow to a culture that is anti-Christ at its core simply because we lack the strength or courage to do otherwise.

In this book, Tom Ascol and Jared Longshore address arguments and attitudes about the topics of science, health, economics, racism, and church and state relations through the lens of Scripture, pushing Christians to reclaim these principles of strength and courage which are so sorely lacking in our context today. God help us.

Rev. Christopher Lee Bolt, Ph.D.
Pastor at Elkton Baptist Church, Elkton, TN

In this book, Tom Ascol and Jared Longshore have faithfully sounded the trumpet of warning like faithful watchmen on the wall (Ezekiel 33). But they have done more than identify a crafty, encroaching enemy; they have also blown the silver trumpet blast that summons God's people to war (Numbers 10:9). This book is full of practical wisdom that is firmly grounded in God's Word, and the authors write with passion and with muscular clarity. They write like men—men who gladly embrace their God-given masculinity and the responsibility that goes along with it. We have had quite enough of "Be Nice and Inoffensive." We are overflowing with "Be Tolerant and Sensitive." It is high time that we were admonished to "Be Strong and Courageous."

Dr. Jim Scott Orrick
Pastor of the Bullitt Lick Baptist Church, author of *Mere Calvinism* and *Seven Thoughts that Every Christian Ought to Think Every Day: Laying a Foundation for a Life of Prayer*

In this powerful and timely book, Tom Ascol and Jared Longshore offer Christian leaders a bracing, sober, and clear-eyed examination of many cultural challenges facing the church in America—a culture that is increasingly driven by forces of lawlessness, anarchy, and deconstruction. Their clarion call is for the church of Jesus Christ to rise up, overcome her complacency, and boldly fulfill her God-given mission to advance God's kingdom of light into the darkest corners of society.

What marks this book throughout is the deep passion for God and His Word. Ascol and Longshore uphold Jesus Christ is King over all, and His Word in Scripture is our highest authority—not just in the church but over all creation. They provide several practical, biblical recommendations for Christ-followers to live faithfully in the midst of "a crooked and perverse generation, in which you shine as lights in the world" (Phil. 2:15).

Highly recommended!

Scott D. Allen
President of the Disciple Nations Alliance, and author
of *Why Social Justice is Not Biblical Justice: An Urgent
Appeal to Fellow Christians in a Time of Social Crisis*

I found *By What Standard* so useful in defining the jargon of the "woke" movement that I purchased copies for all our students. *Strong and Courageous* takes the next step by equipping believers to react biblically to the "social gospel" heresy.

Dr. Charley Holmes
President, BMA Theological Seminary,
Jacksonville, TX

Christian faithfulness in America requires more of us in the twentieth century than in any previous generation. The advance of liberalism in every public and private sphere now claims many once reliably conservative denominations. These sweeping waves of leftist progressivism were considered revolutionary before, but are seldom detected by the poor standards of contemporary orthodoxy. Both strong and courageous, Tom Ascol and Jared Longshore call Christians to deeper commitment to God's all-sufficient Word and greater confessional clarity for advancement and preservation of the Gospel.

Ryan Helfenbein
Vice President of Communications and Public
Engagement at Liberty University and Executive Director
of the Falkirk Center for Faith & Liberty

Clearing garbage from our hearts so we can see accurately—or should I say, smell truthfully—to clear the garbage from our society is no mean undertaking. This book shows clearly that the living word of revelation containing the soul-saving power of gospel truth has an expansive energy and changes not only believing hearts and church bodies but is intended to be a leaven in society. The authors contend that neither pastors nor the sheep of their flocks can become privatistic or escapist in their pursuit of true piety. They also must be courageous and well informed about the idols within society that challenge the sole authority of the one true God who rules through the victory of Christ over sin, death, the devil, and hell. The dominating idol of self, the unchallenged sense of personal will and prerogative as the chief and only good, expresses itself in many destructive forms: abortion (or the modern expression of Molechism), critical race theory, intersectionality, atheistic and secularistic commitments as the foundation of education, lawlessness of aggressive destruction claimed as a right, movements toward political tyranny, and actions that intrude without warrant on the religious liberties of the people.

This book gives careful attention in each chapter to the gospel and the way its central truths challenge each of these paths to self-destruction. There is no diminishing the importance of reaching heaven at last, but how the gospel informs our steps along the way in this world receives creative and forceful attention. The authors explore the tension between obeying God rather than men while being subject to the governing authorities. They induce thinking about how the Christian should honor the governing officials that God has given us while we take seriously the task of pressing and educating them to see that they are finally responsible to God and his law. This book might not warm the heart, but it will press the mind to engage in some real heart work, attaining a life characterized by truth-informed courage.

Tom J. Nettles
Author, Church Historian,
Retired Professor of Church History and Historical Theology
at the Southern Baptist Theological Seminary, Louisville, KY

Through the centuries, the greatest challenges to the church have always come from within, and so it is with today's American church. Threatened from without by an increasingly hostile culture and a government some have weaponized to advance a progressive agenda, the greatest threat to the church nonetheless comes from those within her ranks who would repurpose the gospel, not as means of radical personal transformation and salvation through the person of Jesus Christ but as a tool to serve earthly gods who cannot save and whose broken promises are a matter of historical record. In *Strong and Courageous*, Tom Ascol and Jared Longshore expose this fraud for what it is: a subtle, pernicious heresy whose seductive nature threatens to rent the church asunder. This is a handbook, a manual for the modern American evangelical. Read it and understand the difference between being "woke"and being awakened.

Larry Alex Taunton
Executive Director of the Fixed Point Foundation, freelance columnist, and author of *The Faith of Christopher Hitchens: The Restless Soul of the World's Most Notorious Atheist.*

The church today faces a clash with culture that demands a robust theology rooted in a submission to the whole counsel of God's Word. As aliens and exiles, whose true citizenship is in the kingdom of God, Christians must understand how to live under God-ordained human authority without compromising our ultimate allegiance to our true King, the Lord Jesus Christ. Tom Ascol and Jared Longshore perform a great service to the church by carefully expounding the theology that is needed for such a time as this. This book needs to be in the hands of every pastor to help navigate his church during the difficult days that most certainly lie ahead.

Tom Buck
Senior Pastor at First Baptist Church of Lindale, TX

Tom Ascol, PhD, has been the Senior Pastor of Grace Baptist Church in Cape Coral, Florida since 1986. He is the President of Founders Ministries and of the Institute of Public Theology and can be heard weekly on the Sword and the Trowel podcast. He and his wife, Donna, have six children, three sons-in-law, a daughter-in-law, and fourteen grandchildren.

Jared Longshore, PhD, is the Associate Pastor of Grace Baptist Church in Cape Coral, Florida and Vice President of Founders Ministries. He is the author of *Wisdom for Kings and Queens* and can be heard weekly on the Sword and the Trowel podcast. He serves as Vice President and Dean of the Institute of Public Theology. Jared and his wife, Heather, have seven children.

STRONG AND COURAGEOUS

FOLLOWING JESUS AMID THE RISE OF AMERICA'S NEW RELIGION

Strong and Courageous

Following Jesus Amid the Rise of America's New Religion

Tom Ascol and Jared Longshore

FOUNDERS
MINISTRIES
CAPE CORAL, FLORIDA

Strong and Courageous
Following Jesus Amid the Rise of America's New Religion

Published by
Founders Press

P.O. Box 150931 • Cape Coral, FL • 33915
Phone: (888) 525-1689
Electronic Mail: officeadmin@founders.org
Website: www.founders.org
©2020 Founders Press
Printed in the United States of America

ISBN: 978-1-943539-24-6

Cover Design by Jaye Bird LLC
Interior Design by InkSmith Editorial Services

With gratitude to God for the privilege of serving Him together, we dedicate this book to our fellow elders, Jorge Alvarez, Chris Faro, Graham Gunden, and Don Kiah, and to the members of Grace Baptist Church in Cape Coral, Florida.

Soli Deo Gloria.

Contents

ACKNOWLEDGMENTS

This book was more born than written. For the last few years the ideas and convictions set forth here have been forged, debated, tested, and proven in the press of everyday pastoral ministry. We have spent hundreds of hours together discharging our responsibilities to shepherd the wonderful members of Grace Baptist Church. The weight of that stewardship is what ultimately gave rise to this book. In the pages that follow we have simply tried to put into words and organize into chapters the burdens that we have borne in teaching the flock over which the Lord has made us overseers. It is to them, and to our fellow elders with whom we joyfully share that responsibility, that we dedicate this effort.

Far more people have helped get this book out in a timely fashion than we can possibly name, but there are a few who we simply must thank publicly. Mark Coppenger sacrificed time from his busy schedule to provide invaluable feedback with record speed. His observations, suggestions, encouragements, and critiques are a model of brotherly love and have proven so helpful (and often entertaining) that we would gladly write another book just to have the benefit of his edifying input. Jim Orrick made many helpful suggestions that enabled us to say what we meant to say with greater precision and accuracy. Jeff Johnson, Chris Bolt, Tom Buck, and Rebecca Sissons also provided keen insight and help in reading an early draft of the manuscript. All of these exemplify in their respective spheres the kind of strength and courage that we commend in this book, and we are grateful for them.

Finally, we must give special thanks to our wives, Donna and Heather. They have steadily helped us refine our thinking and communication through extensive conversations about the Scriptures and the times. They have also endured some of the heartache and challenges that go with following Jesus in the face of opposition. Courageous and fruitful women they are, laughing at the time to come and dining at the table that the Lord has prepared in the presence of enemies. Without their help and joyful sacrifice, this book would have never been written.

Obviously, the mistakes and deficiencies that remain are ours and no one else's. Our hope and prayer is that what we have written will help God's people to stand firm in the evil day (Ephesians 6:13).

Tom Ascol & Jared Longshore
December 2, 2020
Cape Coral, Florida

PREFACE

A dozen or so years ago, John MacArthur came to Southern Seminary to speak, and I had occasion to thank him for the great help he'd been to me in 1984, when, as a new pastor, I found myself in a squall of dismay and opposition to my policy on divorce and remarriage. I'd stumbled into it as I was teaching through that year's January Bible Study on 1 Corinthians. Chapter 7 touched on the issue, and, with the observation that I wouldn't feel free to officiate at some weddings, the honeymoon was over.

I was swamped with literature (e.g., William Barclay and Loftin Hudson); agonizing first-person testimony ("Divorce is like dying"; "I just want my little girl to be happy"); rhetorical questions ("Are you saying it's the unforgivable sin?"; "How do you think you'll minister to them in the future?"); the counsel of prudence ("You don't want to get out too far in front of your people, or they'll mistake you for the enemy"; "With people leaving, it's not clear how we're going to be able to pay your salary"); counter-texting ("Genesis says that it's not good for man to be alone"); experiential demonstrations

("But he's blessed our marriage with great kids"); accusatory comparisons ("Our former pastor didn't draw those lines, and neither do many other prominent pastors"); the classic stylistic scorecard ("It wasn't what you said but the way you said it"); and some good old *ad hominem* ("Well, you're just not loving").

About two months into this, I headed out for Army Reserve duty in the Mojave Desert, and, just before I left, a friendly deacon handed me a cassette with a message on the topic by John MacArthur, of whom I was only vaguely aware. Still reeling from the conflict and some measure of self-doubt, I was suddenly taken by MacArthur's calm, confident, and biblically reasonable case for limits on remarriage. Talk about a Balm in Gilead. Maybe I wasn't callous after all. Maybe I was in the biblical ballpark. Maybe I hadn't disqualified myself from the "Christlike" pastorate.

Little did I know when I thanked John on campus, decades after his desert ministry to my soul, that I would be thanking him for brand new heroics in 2020. I didn't suspect that he would be standing tall (or even need to be) in the midst of various madnesses besetting evangelicals in this era—a concatenation of social justice, critical race theory, intersectionality, COVID tyranny, and PR idolatry.

Neither did I suspect that Founders Ministries would be taking the lead among Southern Baptists in holding the fort and advancing against the woke conceits that had beguiled many of our leaders. From my seminary days, I knew Tom Ascol as one who urged respect for and faithfulness to the theology of such forebears as John Broadus and Basil Manly, from whose names we got Broadman Press (the B in B&H). But there he was, speaking truth to the power, the powerful forces assuring us that all was well in the fold, grandees disposed to bark, "How dare you, Sir! Move on. Nothing to see here."

But there was something big to see, and Tom didn't shrink from pointing it out. And it wasn't a one-off proposition, but a faithful crusade against what I call a legion of "sensitivity thugs." ("If you don't accommodate, yea venerate, our feelings, we will crush you.") Steady, steady, he and Jared Longshore have courageously and thoughtfully helped us sort things out, often through *The Sword and The Trowel* podcast.

One doesn't have to agree with everything they conclude to see that they have set us an excellent table. (For instance, I'm not all in with the "regulative principle.") And from that table of discourse, they have brought generous helpings of wisdom to this book—well-seasoned, nutritious fare.

It's said that we academically/culturally insecure Southern Baptists used to strike a bargain with our liberal theological "betters"—"We'll call you Christians if you'll call us scholars." Now, it seems that a host of ecclesiastical adepts, young and old, have retooled the arrangement to read, "We'll call you deeply insightful if you call us likeable." A fool's game, one that Tom and Jared refuse to play.

Mark Coppenger

Introduction

SECULAR AMERICA AND THE NEED FOR A DEEPER REFORMATION

"What in the world is going on? What has happened to our nation?" Many American Christians are asking questions like these at the moment. Granted, 2020 has been an election year. But this is not just another crazy political moment. We are watching the civil expression of an inner and erroneous faith commitment. That secular faith, expressed in the Social Justice movement, is committed to a law, a gospel, and a particular vision of our world's future structure. But it is not committed to God's law, Christ's gospel, or the future that will most surely come about by the work of the Holy Spirit. Regrettably, America is in trouble, in part because the secularists have been much more committed to their faith than Christians have been to the true faith.

What we see forming in America is both a theological and political movement. All of life is theological. You do not get away from God. You do not get away from being religious. Man has been created in the image of God and is going to worship something or someone. The new religion maintains deeply held convictions about the nature of the world, humanity, ethics, justice, love, and mercy. Those convictions have been put on display in the rioting, protesting, and calls for the deconstruction of our society. While both the root and fruit are erroneous, the movement is nevertheless doctrinally informed and politically focused.

The message of this secular faith includes that America must be overthrown. Western Civilization is an evil that must be disassembled. Christianity, they say, is draped in whiteness, complete with a white Jesus and white theology. Good Christians hear that and say, "Oh, I don't want to be a racist." So, there is a concerted effort to get rid of all of the whiteness. The hope is that once all of that abominable whiteness is purged from among us, then the holy seed will remain. Sadly, many churches, even good evangelical churches, are being manipulated and drawn into bad paths by such logic.

Many Christians have become complicit in the agenda of this secular faith. They say, "How wrong we have been about everything! This horrible nation was birthed in irredeemable sin. Seeing how wrong we have been, we need to sit down, be quiet, and listen." Others have sought to avoid these matters. They say, "I don't understand these things. I'm just going to be quiet."

To our fellow Christians, and especially pastors, our message is that the time for silence is gone. We must be willing to speak what God has said in His Word, and we must do so boldly, clearly, unapologetically, and lovingly. Our call is not to save America. We are grateful for our nation and lament to see the trajectory of our civil life. We do not want to see our nation unnecessarily destroyed. But our concerns are much deeper than the fate of a single nation. We are speaking out because there are false teachers among us who are advancing ideas that will lead people to hell.

HARDENED SECULARISM

Secularism, in a sense, is inept. It cannot sustain a civilization. Christianity, on the other hand, can. History illustrates how societies flourish when they adopt Christian principles. Islam also has some sustaining power. While it does not have the same strength as Christianity, Islam can undergird some kind of civic life. Secularism, however, tends to fall flat.

Even so, while secularism may not have what it takes to build civilization, it sure seems to have what it takes to tear it down. Vain philosophies can do a great deal of civil damage when they harden. As long as your secularism is soft, merely an idea floating in your mind, then you won't torch too many businesses. But ideas have consequences. Eventually, the rubber of your ideas meets the road of life. That gripping point is Critical Theory[1] and all of its various offshoots. That unpleasing aroma of burnt rubber and burning local businesses, is the Social Justice movement in all of its forms.

Christians must come to see the religious nature of secularism with its sacrament of Critical Social Justice. Until they do, they will misunderstand the times and be ill-equipped to

---

1 Timon Cline has wisely said, "Though myriad intellectual strands have come together to form contemporary critical theory—indeed, one of the chief characteristics of critical theory generally is that it is allergic to rigid definition—most agree that the Frankfurt School and the development of western or cultural (or some prefer "humanist") Marxism—Marxist framework applied critique of western culture— played a foundational role in this origin story." For a deeper analysis of Critical Theory see: Timon Cline, "Identity Politics and the Bondage of the Will," *Founders Journal* 118, (Fall 2019): https://founders.org/2020/02/10/identity-politics-and-the-bondage-of-the-will.

live wisely in them. For example, if you have a neighbor who is a Jehovah's Witness, most Christians will have no problem with you saying to him, "What you do is wrong. What you believe is wrong. Your worship is wrong. Jesus is God." Many will commend you for speaking the truth. But if you have an LGBTQ couple next door flying the rainbow flag, you will not be commended for telling them, "What you are doing is wrong. What you are committed to is wrong. What you believe is wrong. Jesus is God."

We see the faulty religion of Jehovah's Witnesses, but we do not see the LGBTQ community, the Black Lives Matter movement, or the proponents of Cultural Marxism as practicing a false religion.[2] Many fail to see these as actual faith commitments that will lead people to hell. The book *By What Standard* explores this idea in more detail. The introduction states,

> Many have failed to see that a false religion is afoot... This false religion is the same one God gave people up to in Romans 1. We have turned from worshiping the Creator to worshiping the creature. This religious system teaches that man is God and that the human will is the holy standard. Salvation masquerades as that future state of universal equality attained by strict adherence to the Hegelian dialectic. But, in reality, it consists of satiating the unrestricted human appetite by any means necessary.
>
> So we do not leap upon altars crying out to Baal to send fire while cutting ourselves. But we do leap up on cars as we riot in fiery streets, cutting down people's

---

2   For an introduction to Cultural Marxism see: Voddie Bauchum, "Cultural Marxism," Founders Ministries, January 3, 2019, https://founders.org/sermons/cultural-marxism.

livelihoods while crying out to finite, governmental gods. We do not sacrifice our children to Molech, but we do sacrifice them to Planned Parenthood.[3]

A King Like the Secular Nations

Godless kings do not limit their government. Some people maintain that the secular king will not burden them with a heavy yoke of legislation. Those same people believe that a God-fearing king would weigh them down with undesirable religious standards. But that set up is altogether backward. It is the king who fears the Lord that dawns upon men like a new day—"When one rules justly over men, ruling in the fear of God, he dawns on them like the morning light, like the sun shining forth on a cloudless morning, like rain that makes grass to sprout from the earth" (2 Samuel 23:3-4).

Much of the COVID pandemic response in 2020 gave us a vivid reminder of this principle. California governor Gavin Newsom, for example, prohibited restaurants from opening in the summer. He also issued an order mandating churches not to sing or chant when they gathered. Perhaps the governor is genuinely concerned about the virus. For the sake of argument, let us give him the benefit of the doubt and say he was doing what he believed to be best for his state. Even so, what is happening here?

A governmental authority is telling Christians what they can and cannot do in worship. They can still gather; they just cannot sing. Tragically, the typical response has been pastors saying, "Romans 13, Romans 13, the governor says that we must not sing so we will not sing." Have we forgotten that

---

3 Jared Longshore, *By What Standard? God's World, God's Rules* (Cape Coral, FL: Founders Press, 2020), v.

we, and Governor Newsom, are people under the authority of Christ? When governors begin to dictate what the church can and cannot do, those of us who believe the Bible must come back and say, "Wait a minute, we already have dictates on what we can and cannot do in worship. Those orders are found in the Scripture."

Those who come out of the Protestant, Reformed, Confessional background argue for the regulative principle in worship. We are not free to do whatever we want to do in worship. We have a book, and God has spoken. The Second Commandment demonstrates that God takes very seriously how He is approached in worship. We see that in the practice of the Lord's Supper. In 1 Corinthians 11, we hear that God killed people for inappropriate attendance of the Lord's Supper. He killed Nadab and Abihu in the Old Testament because they offered up strange fire, contrary to what He had prescribed.

So we have a divine prescription. If the governor thinks he can prohibit what God has commanded, then he has gotten out of his lane. He has been called upon by God as a civil magistrate to operate in a way that promotes what is good and punishes what is evil. Given the ill-conceived mandate of Governor Newsom, Christians were forced to obey God or Governor Newsom. The problem belongs not to the Christians in California, but to the governor of California. As Samuel Rutherford once said, "Truth to Christ cannot be treason to Caesar."[4]

Here again, we are reminded that it is not whether, but which. It is not whether you will have faith, but which kind

---

4 Samuel Rutherford, *Lex, Rex: The Law And The King* (Moscow, ID: Canon Press, 2020), 1.

of faith are you going to have? Are you going to have the Christian faith? Or are you going to have the secular faith?

In 1 Samuel 23, Saul is chasing David, trying to kill him. Throughout that chapter, David continues to inquire of the Lord. David discovers that the Philistines are attacking Keilah, a city in Israel. David prays, "God, should I go and fight them?" God replies, "Yes, go fight them." Saul, meanwhile, pursues David. While Saul acquires data, he does not inquire of the Lord. However, hearing that Saul pursues him, David prays, "God, should I flee?" God says, "Yes, flee." David flees to the wilderness of Ziph. The Ziphites go to Saul and say, "David is with us." Saul's reply is quite humorous. He tells the Ziphites to make more sure. "David is sneaky," Saul says, "so bring me solid intelligence." But, Saul does not inquire of the Lord. He pursues David, but David escapes.

Saul fails to deal with the God who exists. He was remarkably diligent with getting precise information. But, he cared nothing for God's Word on the matter. There is nothing wrong with getting sure data. All truth is God's truth. We should pursue it anywhere we can find it. The problem with Saul is that he wanted to get the information apart from faith in God. He trusted himself rather than his Creator.

In California, there is the "king like the nations" with all of his COVID predictions. He is not dealing with God or thinking about what God has revealed in His Word. He is not concerned with how God says to operate in the world. But he can clearly see that, because of the data, the church cannot sing in California.

We have had contact with pastors in California who are full of courage and joy. They have taken an altogether different approach. They are resolved to follow Christ. One fellow pastor said, "I'm going to sing. And if I die from singing and catching COVID, you just tell everybody that I'd rather sing and die than live and not sing."

A HERITAGE OF FAITHFULNESS

That kind of pastoral leadership is anything but secular. It is full of faith in God and love toward people. There is something light about such godly leadership. Christ said, "Come to me, all who labor and are heavy laden, and I will give you rest. Take my yoke upon you, and learn from me, for I am gentle and lowly in heart, and you will find rest for your souls. For my yoke is easy, and my burden is light" (Matthew 11:28-30).

We have glorious examples of such leadership throughout church history. Caesar said, "You cannot worship anybody but Caesar." The Conventicle Act in 17th century England prohibited assemblies. Our brothers and sisters in parts of Africa and China have often suffered from tyranny. Their response was not to go along with whatever unrighteous statute was handed down. They obeyed God rather than men (Acts 5:29). We look to these faithful Christians and stand on their shoulders. We praise God for their faith. Many went to their deaths. They were burned. They were hung. They were drowned because they determined to honor God.

Sometimes we look back on those stories and think everyone knew that the Christians had the moral high ground; their oppressors were real devilish people. But when the oppression happens in real-time, things are not so clean cut. Those who rule unjustly attempt to grab the moral high ground. When Rome persecuted the early church martyr Polycarp, he was told to repent and cry out, "Away with the atheists!" The problem was, Rome wanted him to repent of his faith in Christ. The atheists, according to Rome, were the Christians who would not worship the emperor. Polycarp responded with courage—"But Polycarp, gazing with a stern countenance on all the multitude of the wicked heathen then in the stadium, and waving his hand towards them, while with groans he looked up to heaven, said, 'Away with the Atheists.'"[5]

THE TOPPLING OF STATUES

Quite a few statues were pulled down in the civil unrest of the year 2020. Those toppled statues send a clear signal. From the vantage point of Social Justice, there is no honoring people who are sinners. The world must be flattened out. Such a maneuver accords with Critical Theory. The goal is a future state of universal equality. All things must be equally shared, and that includes honor. No gold medals, unless everyone gets one. No statues, unless everyone gets one. Some may claim that the statue toppling is only about racism, sexism, or homophobia. But something deeper is going on. They would try to tear down those statues regardless of the issue. They do not desire a level playing field. They desire, or at least pretend to desire, a level award ceremony podium.

But that is not the way Christianity works. Christianity has a place for commending fallen people. The faith, once for all delivered to the saints, commends certain actions and shames others. The secular-religious commitment makes no such distinction. Hardened secularism does shame things like maleness, whiteness, etc. But it does so only because

---

5 Roberts, A., Donaldson, J., & Coxe, A. C. (Eds.). (1885). The Encyclical Epistle of the Church at Smyrna. In *The Apostolic Fathers with Justin Martyr and Irenaeus* (Vol. 1, p. 41). Buffalo, NY: Christian Literature Company.

those identities are seen to have more power than the others. Theoretically, someday out there in the future, once everyone has the same payday, the vitriol for those oppressor identities would be gone.

If you want to adopt the modern *zeitgeist*, you will have to rewrite the Bible. Scripture says to give honor to whom honor is due (Romans 13:7). Is there some sinless person that is being spoken of in that text? Of course not. Look at Solomon, David, Moses, Paul, and Peter. All of these men are teachers from whom we are to learn. Their sins are evident. God does not paper over them. He puts them out there to be seen. Imperfect men receive honor, and the glory of the gospel is displayed.

The gospel provides real salvation for real sinners. All of us have blind spots. All of us have sin that remains in us. The virtue-signaling proponents of the new religion claim they are greater than those who have gone before. That sentiment is the spirit of the age. The church cannot go along with it. We cannot pretend that we are walking together whenever we are operating on two different bases of authority under the lordship of different gods.

A Deeper Reformation

If the church is to move forward in faithfulness to Christ, then we are in need of a deeper reformation. We have seen God work in the past, but some of our past movements have been too shallow. For example, the inerrancy movement among Southern Baptists, beginning in 1979 with the election of Adrian Rogers as SBC president, was a great work that stopped short. The 20th century saw the advance of liberalism in nearly every denomination. But the Southern

Baptists resolved that God's Word was inerrant. You can hardly find anyone within the Southern Baptist Convention anymore who says the Bible has mistakes in it. Such a statement, however, was not uncommon in Southern Baptist seminaries before the inerrancy movement.

But the inerrancy movement did not go deep enough. We must not only affirm that the Bible is inerrant; we must actually read what is in it. We are not permitted to pay superficial service to the text of Scripture, pretending that it can be harmonized with every thought and imagination of man. The sword of the Spirit divides. In many cases, Southern Baptists have cared far too much about the praise of man to speak plainly the words of Scripture.

Another movement, which had many good aspects, was the Young Restless and Reformed movement. This movement was resolved to glorify Christ and held to Calvinistic soteriology. Large numbers of young people began to identify as Calvinists. T-shirts reading "Jonathan Edwards is my homeboy" were in vogue. We praise God for much that happened. But we have seen that the Young Restless and Reformed movement was not deep enough either. They had a godly ambition but failed to ground themselves in God's Word.

In *Pilgrim's Progress*, John Bunyan describes Mr. By-Ends who loves religion when it walks in silver slippers. That is what happened with many in both of these movements. It became practical to be an inerrantist, and it became cool to be a Calvinist. It is not that they were duplicitous in their thinking. Instead, there was simply a lack of resolve to take up the cross.

DOCTRINAL RECOVERY

Along with a resolve to go with Christ outside the camp, we need to recover certain doctrines and methods that have been lost. While we only have space for sketching the general direction, getting an idea of the doctrinal work required is critical to the work of reformation.

Law and Gospel

We desperately need a recovery of law and gospel. James Henley Thornwell was right when he said,

> The Gospel, like its blessed Master, is always crucified between two thieves—legalists of all sorts on the one hand and Antinomians on the other; the former robbing the Savior of the glory of his work for us, and the other robbing him of the glory of his work within us.[6]

The new religion has a law, but not God's law. It has a gospel, but not God's gospel. They have an ethic, but it is no Christian ethic. They offer a process through which you can be washed partially clean, but it is not through the blood of the Lamb. That false gospel cannot stand against the true gospel of God. We need only proclaim it. Ernest Reisinger's book, *The Law and The Gospel*, is an excellent place to start to get theologically grounded on this topic.[7]

Confessionalism

We also need a recovery of robust and sound doctrine. We have glorious confessions handed down to us from our

---

6 J. H. Thornwell, "Antinomianism" in *The Collected Writings of James Henley Thornwell* (Richmond, VA: Presbyterian Committee of Publication, 1871), 386.

7 Ernest Reisinger, *The Law and The Gospel* (Cape Coral, FL: Founders Press, 2019).

fathers. Clear articulation of truth does not lead to unnecessary division. Some would avoid specificity in doctrine for the sake of unity. But that pathway never works. We do not need to avoid sound doctrine; we need to avoid pride. A fresh apprehension of the value and usefulness of confessions will strengthen the church against the rise of the new religion and help us maintain biblical orthodoxy. Tom Nettles has produced an excellent book called *Teaching Truth and Training Hearts*, in which he introduces modern Christians to their confessional heritage.[8] The 1689 confession of faith has been translated into modern English.[9] This resource serves as an aid to individuals, families, and church as we seek to recover our confessional commitments.

Pastoral Theology

Along with these recoveries, we need a renewed understanding and commitment to pastoral theology. Pastors are called to shepherd and defend God's flock. We receive regular communications from Christians telling us their churches are being torn apart by the social justice movement. We need to consider once again what is involved in faithful shepherding, preaching, praying, correcting, and encouraging. *Dear Timothy* is a book that details the calling and work of pastors that they might shepherd the flock of God that is among them.[10] It is a timely resource for developing a healthy pastoral theology.

---

8 Tom Nettles, *Teaching Truth and Training Hearts* (Cape Coral, FL: Founders Press, 2017).

9 Stan Reeves, *The 1689 Confession of Faith in Modern English* (Cape Coral, FL: Founders Press, 2012).

10 Tom Ascol, *Dear Timothy: Letters on Pastoral Ministry* (Cape Coral, FL: Founders Press, 2004).

Creation

We need a deeper understanding of creation. Perhaps the most crucial verse in all of the Bible is Genesis 1:1, "In the beginning, God created the heavens and the earth." We are creatures and there is only one Creator. This is God's world. He brought it all into existence and has done so for His own glory. Everything operates under His authority, the way He has determined that it should operate. In order to live well in this world we have to take Him at His word and get in line with what He says.

The doctrine of creation carries many implications. If God created the world, then no place in the world is off-limits from Him. It does not matter if you are in Colorado or Florida. It does not matter if you are married or single. It does not matter if you are fighting a war or in a classroom. It does not matter if you are a president, a legislator, or a judge. Everything is His. Jesus Christ has made all, and He is Lord of all. It also follows that the creation is good. We know it is fallen. Genesis 3 tells the story. But that fall has not utterly obliterated the goodness of creation.

The Physical World

It is important to realize that mankind's rebellion has not destroyed the goodness of the physical world. God gave us bodies. Therefore, our physical bodies are good. Life in this world, in both its spiritual and physical dimensions, is good. We indeed are seated with Christ in the heavenly places. He created the heavens. But we are also very much still living on earth before death and we must not disdain this life or the physical realities that it entails.

The secular mindset sees death as natural and universal. We all experience death. We see that it is inevitable. But death is not natural. It is an invader, an intruder. Paul calls it the last enemy (1 Corinthians 15:26). At a Christian funeral, we praise God for the life that was lived, but it is right that we also grieve. Whenever we consider death we should stop and think, "An enemy has done this" (Matthew 13:28).

Christians have marching orders from Jesus. Those orders are to make disciples of all nations, baptizing them in the name of the Father, Son, and Spirit. We are to teach people to observe all that Jesus has commanded. At the funeral of a fellow-believer, we remember that one more soldier has finished the battle, and we carry on with the task assigned to us.

The Great Commission maintains a very earthly component. We see it in Jesus, announcing that He has all authority in heaven and on earth. The apostles were told to go and make disciples of all nations. We can see the earthly component to the Lord's Prayer as well. Jesus said we are to pray, "your kingdom come, your will be done, on earth as it is in heaven" (Matthew 6:10). There is a physical component to the Great Commission because God saves people body and soul. There are physical implications of God's kingdom, for when His will is done on earth, it is done by people who are both physical and spiritual.

A misunderstanding of the spiritual and physical can result in all sorts of trouble. Such misunderstanding was revealed through the year 2020 with the panic that resulted from the COVID pandemic. It was also seen through the violent protests, rioting, and looting that took place in the name of "justice." All of our work for Christ must be done by faith. But when we do it by faith, our work will regularly have tangible effects. We do not see the kingdom advance by human will or exertion, but God does use means.

As pastors who serve a local church in Cape Coral, Florida, that reality helped us and our fellow elders shepherd our congregation through that tumultuous year. Jesus has told us to make disciples. That commission could not be forsaken as we dealt with the COVID pandemic. That is why we kept regularly worshiping each Lord's Day (after taking two weeks to heed and assess the state of emergency called by our governmental officials). If the salvation of sinners were not central to the commission we have received from our King, then we would have done several things differently. But, if there really are embodied souls surrounding us who must repent of sin, trust Jesus and obey Him, then that truth determines how we will operate body and soul.

Metaphysics

We need a recovery of the true nature of reality. What is real? According to Karl Marx, the only thing that exists is the material world. Christians, however, believe in the physical and the spiritual. Spiritual things are not pretend things or imaginary things. Angels are just as real as plywood. The mainstream media, as well as certain governmental, medical, and religious leaders, served up steady doses of fear during the COVID pandemic of 2020. We were encouraged to put our hope in a vaccine, or a mask, or six feet of distance. Certainly, we are happy to commend staying home when sick, and we should all be thankful for such ready access to helpful medicines. But, we ought not forget that God once stopped a plague by telling an angel to stop killing people (2 Samuel 24:16). Too many Christians have been all about virus-avoiding tactics with little or no, "Lord have mercy."

Why has this been the case? Because we are often rank materialists when it comes to our conception of reality. The truth, however, is that reality is more than the material world. Reality is defined by the God who made it. What is love? What is justice? What is truth? What is mercy? These realities, just as certainly as physical creatures, are what God says that they are. We are observing a present attempt to drain all of those words of their substance. This is nothing less than an effort to twist and pervert reality. But this attempt to hijack God's things will not work.

God told Moses, "I AM WHO I AM. ... Say this to the people of Israel: 'I AM has sent me to you'" (Exodus 3:14). When we live aware of this fundamental truth, then all of life falls into place. If we get a vaccine from the doctor, we pray, "God, make this vaccine work." If we have surgery, "Lord, help the surgeon to use all the skills you have given him and make the surgery work." If you cannot get to a doctor or do not have access to medicine, God has not changed. We ought not to be presumptuous, but He can work apart from means. If you drink a cup of coffee, you are likely going to feel a bit more energetic because it has caffeine. The wonder is that God gives you the energy every time you drink coffee. You get a good night of sleep, and you feel better. But where in the world did that come from? God did it again. We do not live in a materialistic and mechanistic universe. There is order, indeed. But the order is maintained by Jesus Christ, who "upholds the universe by the word of his power" (Hebrews 1:3).

With this mindset, you are positioned to enjoy creation without worshiping it. God's sunsets blow us away, but we do not worship the sun. We worship the God who made the sun, not the sun itself as a god. We do this because of the Creator-creature distinction. God is eternal. Creation is not God, but it is dependent on Him. So we can enjoy the gift and worship the Giver.

The Advance of the Kingdom of Christ

Too many churches seem to function with a malnourished sense of the kingdom of Christ. They have lost their eschatological vision. They might say, "Well, no, we still have it." But, compare the action of such churches to the Black Lives Matter riots. Who is more passionate about getting their gospel out? The Black Lives Matter movement and the social justice warriors who support it, or those Evangelical Christians who automatically and passively acquiesced to governmental edicts in 2020? Far too many Christians said, "The emperor said not to gather. Therefore, we are not gathering." The Black Lives Matter people said, "We have a mission. We have an eschatological vision for what we want to see happen." They assembled. They proclaimed. May God awaken His people so that we will be more zealous for the cause of our God and His truth than our unbelieving neighbors are for their gods and the lies that fuel their cause. When such reviving power comes, then Christians will stand up and say, "We have a job to do too. So, with all due respect to our proper human authorities, we have marching orders from Christ and must not be deterred from our mission."

A significant problem with American Christianity is that it is more American than Christian. We think the default is, if the emperor says it, then we have to do it. But we must remember that the emperor, like all other creatures, is under the authority of King Jesus. Christians are sojourners and strangers here. We have a King, we have a commission, and we belong to a kingdom. That kingdom is never going to fail. It does not operate like the kingdoms of this world. It must never be equated with the kingdoms of this world. The kingdom of God is spiritual, led by a body and soul resurrected King. God's kingdom is a heavenly kingdom, full of embodied souls, that is coming upon earth as it is in heaven. The work of reformation requires a recovery of the nature and function of this glorious kingdom.

Political Theology

Many people boast in their freedom to speak their minds and stand against injustice. But, freedom of speech arises not from a secular worldview, but a biblilcal one. In the Christian ethic, you have the freedom to harbor and communicate erroneous ideas without getting your head cut off. The physical sword belongs to the civil magistrate to execute judgment on criminals who do evil to their fellow image-bearers. The sword of the Spirit belongs to the church of Jesus Christ. So we persuade, proclaim, and profess, but we do not coerce a person's will. We, instead, proclaim Christ and trust Him to bring about new life.

We are experiencing the crumbling of our nation because the foundations washed away a long time ago. The Judeo-Christian principles that were there, in the beginning, have eroded. The civil magistrate holds the sword for punishing the wrongdoer. The church bears responsibility for reminding the civil magistrate that the sword he holds was given to him by the God of the Bible. Many have simplistically referred to Romans 13, claiming that it teaches de facto obedience to civil authorities. But you do not get to exegete Romans 13 without saying that your governor is a minister of Yahweh, "For the authorities are ministers of God" (Romans 13:6). That does not mean that civil authorities are to establish the exact same statues found in Israel's Old Covenant legislation. But, it does mean that God's servants should obey their master and listen to His instruction to them when they fulfill their duties.

Because we believe the gospel, we believe in the lordship of Christ over every square inch of creation. Nothing is outside of His authority. The sword has been put in the hand of civil authorities by God. The church must be willing to say that. We need to admonish police officers not to brutalize people they are called to defend and serve. We need to commend them for their honorable service. We need to remind governors of their responsibility to promote what is good and punish what is evil.

The Spirit's Work of New Birth

The work of the Spirit remains front and center in our labor for a deeper reformation. If we are going to see things become what they ought to be, if we are to see things biblically reformed, then people must be born again. Only the regenerate trust and obey Jesus. There is this great temptation to pursue reformation in a top-down fashion. But it is not by might nor by power, but rather by the Spirit that these things come about (Zechariah 4:6). We are to trust God's promises. We are to preach. We are to work by faith and pray. All must be done by the power of the Spirit.

Our prayer is that the chapters that follow will aid the church in this work of a deeper reformation so that we might follow Christ amid the rise of America's new religion.

PART 1:

IN THE DEFENSE

1

REJECT FALSE HOPE:
THE LIE OF THE NEW RELIGION

Universal equality and autonomy are the bread and butter of modern thought. The mantra goes: we are accountable to no one, dependent on no one, but must have precisely the same things as everyone else. A false hope is associated with these falsehoods: if you will simply be your independent self, and abide by the principle of universal equality, then all will be well. We will all gather downtown, hold hands, and sing *Kumbaya* as one big happy group of independent individuals. This false hope appeared in the wake of the death of Supreme Court Justice Ruth Bader Ginsburg.

Many Christians spoke glowingly of Justice Ginsburg while acknowledging disagreements with her over abortion. They say she was a wonderful example and leader, even though she got the abortion issue wrong. The problem is she was wrong on abortion because she was wrong on autonomy and equality. Anyone who would say she was a great advocate for women's rights must, of course, deal with her approval of all of the murdered women in the womb. When it comes to the understanding of life, death, equality, self-governance, womanhood, and justice, the Christian positions and Justice Ginsburg's positions are as oil and water.

No Grace Without Heaven

On the night of Ruth Bader Ginsburg's death, American citizens gathered on the steps of the Supreme Court Building in Washington D.C. Beneath the engraved words "Equal Justice Under Law," they sang John Lennon's *Imagine*, a song which subverts the very pillars upon which such a notion stands. His song is an anthem of the East, one that cannot be harmonized with the Christian faith.

Lennon implores us to imagine there is no heaven above us and no hell below us. He reassures us that it is easy to imagine this if you try. Before we take Lennon's advice, we should consider that a gazelle can imagine no lion. It may even be easy for the gazelle to imagine the lion is not there. But it is not very smart. The same goes for heaven and hell. God has determined that heaven and hell exist. Autonomous man claims he can imagine away what God has established. But God says, "Where were you when I laid the foundation of the earth? Tell me, if you have understanding" (Job 38:4).

In the attempt to erase heaven and earth lives the impulse to reject "the binary." But, the Christian system is full of the binary. Creation itself is marked by the binary. There is light and darkness, land and sea, sun and moon, man and woman. Creation points to the ultimate binary, God and not God, or God and creation. But Lennon imagines no countries so that we can share the world. He goes so far as to dream of no possessions whatsoever. We assume that would include his song, so perhaps we can remove his name from it. The dream maintains that once the binary is gone, the world will live as one.

Imagine is the worship song sung by those who possess the false hope of equality and autonomy. When we hear the word autonomy, we often think of the autonomous individual. When we think of equality, we assume you need two individuals who are equal in some sense. But when equality must be universal, when you must have an equal amount of everything, you end up being identical. If you are identical, then you are no longer two, but one in every sense. This new humanistic and holistic oneness, attained by removing possessions and borders, cannot have another entity outside itself standing over it. The whole lot of humanity must be autonomous. God must go. The lie is that we can do such a thing and maintain love and peace. That is the false hope of universal equality and autonomy.

Such an anthem, sung on the steps of the Supreme Court, is troubling enough. But things got worse that evening as the group followed *Imagine* with John Newton's *Amazing Grace.* Grace comes down from the heavens, but Lennon has erased them. Grace implies that someone gives you something you do not have, but Lennon has said there are no possessions. Grace involves receiving help from outside of yourself. But, autonomous man is not allowed to do such a thing. He cannot do such a thing because we are all now one in every sense, so there is no other being from whom we might receive help.

While there can be no peace between *Imagine* and *Amazing Grace*, syncretism is precisely what is being attempted. The combination of these two songs is a troubling example of what is happening in certain evangelical churches. There is an attempt to blend Lennon's vision and Newton's vision, the secular faith and the Christian faith, the false hope and the blessed hope (Titus 2:13).

Observing the False Hope

Remarkably, the same people sang both of those conflicting songs on the steps of the Supreme Court of the United States. The attempt to harmonize those songs illustrates the religious impulse even within people who claim they want no religion. We have an opportunity to see how you can gut Christian concepts of their Christianity while still using the vernacular. When the arc of a particular culture is away from its Christian heritage, you face the problem of singing your father's song without the actual content. *Amazing Grace,* however, like the Constitution, is not a living document that we can twist to say whatever we want it to mean.

For example, when Newton wrote that amazing grace saved a wretch like him, he referred to his rebellion against God. God says, "None is righteous, no, not one; no one understands; no one seeks for God. All have turned aside; together they have become worthless; no one does good, not even one" (Romans 3:10-12). Humanity's wretchedness arises from humanity's sin. We identify sin according to God's law, "Sin is lawlessness" (1 John 3:4). Newton was wretched because he transgressed God's law. He broke the Ten Commandments.

The secularists sing about wretchedness, too. They use the same word, but a different dictionary. They do not believe we are wretches because we have broken divine law. Humanity is wretched because we have transgressed humanity's autonomous will. We have not been true to ourselves. In recent days, you are a wretch if you violate the standard that a woman has a right to kill her baby. You are a wretch because you think it is fine if human beings are not equal in every sense. You are a wretch if you say that a woman should submit to her husband (Ephesians 5:22). You are a wretch if you believe fathers should raise their children in the discipline and instruction of the Lord (Ephesians 6:4). For that matter, you are a wretch if you say children should obey their parents (Ephesians 6:1). Such relational duties run roughshod over the false hope of autonomy.

Similarly, when Newton sang that he was once blind, but now he sees, he referred to Christian conversion. Conversion involves repenting of sin and trusting in Jesus Christ. It includes having the veil of ignorance removed so that we see the light of the gospel of Jesus Christ (2 Corinthians 4:4).

The secularists can sing of moving from blindness to sight as well. But, here again, they use the Christian lyric without the Christian definition. For them, to move from blindness to sight is to get woke: "I was blind to the oppression that women were facing, but now I see. I was blind to how people were transgressing upon my self-sufficiency, but now I see that I am an independent person."

Newton looked to the new heavens and new earth when he said, "When we've been there ten thousand years, bright shining as the sun, we've no less days to sing God's praise than when we'd first begun." He understood that our never-ending praise would require God making all things new. Therefore, He will be the one we praise forever.

The secularists can sing the same line, but they import an entirely different meaning. They believe they are the ones who will, without divine aid, bring in the glorious day. For them, the God of the Bible is not eternal. But the religious impulse within longs for someone to go on forever. So while the secularists have no hope in the resurrection or a literal new heavens and earth ushered in by God, they imagine humanity's long march toward a golden age on earth where they will sing the praise of the creature forevermore.

That is a false hope. David was right, "Vain is the salvation of man" (Psalm 60:11).

ABORTION: THE FRUITLESSNESS OF AUTONOMY

Ruth Bader Ginsburg was made in the image of God. She paved several trails. By common grace, the Justice developed intellectual and argumentation skills. Yet she spent those good gifts fighting against God, most notoriously in the advocacy of abortion. On that issue, Justice Ginsburg once wrote,

> I appreciate the intense divisions of opinion on the moral question and recognize that abortion today cannot fairly be described as nothing more than birth control delayed. The conflict, however, is not simply one between a fetus' interests and a woman's interests, narrowly conceived... Also in the balance is a woman's autonomous charge of her full life's course—as Professor Kasrst put it, her ability to stand in relation to man, society, and the state as an independent, self-sustaining, equal citizen.[1]

It is a striking admission to say that abortion is more than birth control delayed. Birth control prevents the fertilization of an egg. It prevents the conception of a child, a being created in God's image. Justice Ginsburg has admitted that abortion is the taking of a child's life. She admits that the child in the womb, whom the Justice calls a fetus, has interests. Trees

---

1 Ruth Bader Ginsburg, "Some Thoughts on Autonomy and Equality in Relation to Roe v. Wade." *North Carolina Law Review* 63 (1985): 383.

do not have interests. Rocks do not have interests. People do. She even goes so far as to admit that, in abortion, the child's interests are in "conflict" with the mother's interests. Her point is not that there is no conflict. Her point is that the conflict is not just the baby's interests in conflict with the mother's interests "narrowly conceived."

The baby has much more to battle against if she would not be murdered. She is in conflict with her mother's autonomy and zealous pursuit of equality in relation to man. The wickedness of these words cannot be described. But the logic is not hard to identify, "You desire and do not have, so you murder" (James 4:2).

Hopefully, it is clear why Christians have no place to say that Justice Ginsburg was a great woman. One of our major problems is Christian leaders who make the mistake of showing honor where it is not due. For one reason or another, there is a strong and present tendency to use words that people will like to hear while vacating them of their true meaning. For example, speaking of Justice Ginsburg, Albert Mohler, president of the Southern Baptist Theological Seminary, said that Christians "ought to recognize and respect her courage."[2] Christians indeed should acknowledge the worth and dignity of Justice Ginsburg as a woman created in the image of God. But, it is the progressive, feminist left that thinks Ruth Bader Ginsburg was courageous. That very distorted notion of courage is what results in the slaughter of the unborn.

Far from being courageous, we cannot think of anything more cowardly than murdering an innocent child against

---

2 Albert Mohler, "The Death of Justice Ruth Bader Ginsburg and the Future of the Supreme Court," Albert Mohler, September 19, 2020, https://albertmohler.com/2020/09/19/the-death-of-justice-ruth-bader-ginsburg-and-the-future-of-the-supreme-court.

her interest so that you might maintain your "autonomous charge" of your "full life's course." Justice Ginsburg's notion of women's rights and advancement is driven by ignorance and pride, fueled by the blood of innocent children, and will result only in despair.

Much of our American evangelicalism has become so pragmatic that we think we can have the function without the organ. We believe we can have courage without faith, bravery without the Spirit, and victory without God. Ruth Bader Ginsburg has been better at teaching us her religion than we have at teaching her ours. She has told young women in our nation that they must weigh their children's interests in the scales against their autonomy.

THE ASEITY OF GOD

The heart of the problem with such encouragement is that it is encouragement to be God. The Christian doctrine of divine aseity teaches that God alone is self-sufficient. We are not self-existent. We are not self-sustaining, men nor women. God is independent; we are dependent upon Him. We have no existence apart from Him. We will not sustain ourselves if He does not give us what we need. We certainly do not control our full life's course. If you buy into the current foundational errors on these points, you will end up, like our nation, with millions of murdered innocents.

R.C. Sproul was a great defender of the aseity of God. He once said,

> We have the idea of self-existence or what we call in
> theology, the concept of aseity. When I see that word
> on a blackboard, when I see it in a textbook, I know
> that the vast majority of people in the pew have never

heard of the word. And it is so obscure and esoteric; they don't care about hearing about the word. But I have to tell you, honestly and personally, [when] I see that word, I get chills up my spine. Because in that one little word is captured all of the glory of the perfection of God's being. What makes God different from you and me, and different from the stars, the earthquakes, and any creaturely thing, is that God and God alone has aseity. God and God alone exists by his own power.[3]

What is so offensive about the false hope of autonomy? It dishonors the one and only God who is self-existent and self-sufficient. In place of God, man is set up to be worshiped. As Paul said,

> For although they knew God, they did not honor him as God or give thanks to him, but they became futile in their thinking, and their foolish hearts were darkened. Claiming to be wise, they became fools, and exchanged the glory of the immortal God for images resembling mortal man and birds and animals and creeping things.
>
> Therefore God gave them up in the lusts of their hearts to impurity, to the dishonoring of their bodies among themselves, because they exchanged the truth about God for a lie and worshiped and served the creature rather than the Creator, who is blessed forever! Amen (Romans 1:21-25).

---

3 R. C. Sproul, "God Alone Has Aseity," YouTube, Ligonier Ministries, January 10, 2018. https://www.youtube.com/watch?v=s3VgaRdY5dQ.

THE FOLLY OF AUTONOMY

When people turn from worshiping the Creator to worshiping the creature, God gives them up to foolish hearts and debased minds. They do what ought not to be done. The picture of mother and child is the very foundation of civilization. Anyone looking at that picture with a right mind says, "That is important. Don't mess with that. We won't be around for long if that goes haywire." But, when we worship the creature, we end up doing things that are contrary to nature. We end up making it legal for mothers to murder their children.

General revelation teaches us that we are not autonomous. The apostle Paul explained, "woman is not independent of man nor man of woman; for as woman was made from man, so man is now born of woman" (1 Corinthians 11:11-12). The notion of an autonomous woman dishonors women. It is, moreover, inconceivable. Woman came from man, and she makes man. Both creation and providence demonstrate the folly of autonomy. A woman's body carries another human being. You don't have to have a Ph.D. to see that woman is not autonomous. The baby depends upon the life of the mother. Even after the baby is born, the woman's body produces the milk the baby needs.

THE FOLLY OF UNIVERSAL EQUALITY

God has made man and woman equal in the sense that they are both created in the image of God (Genesis 1:27). But He has certainly not made them equal in every sense of the word. Some would claim that we are straw-manning the secular agenda. They would argue that no one advocates for equality in every sense of the word. The transgender movement, however, says otherwise. The feminist movement has come into significant conflict with the transgender movement, particularly over women's sports. But the transgender movement has simply carried the feminist notion of equality all the way through. While even Justice Ginsburg herself acknowledged inherent differences between men and women, the feminist idea of equality has always included a view to men. When the question comes, "In what sense do you want women to be equal to men?" the response has generally been, "In whatever sense a person wants." The equality is determined, not by an objective standard, but by subjectivity, ability, and desire. The folly of equality is seen in a 1996 Supreme Court case regarding the Virginia Military Institute (VMI).

In the majority opinion, Justice Ginsburg found VMI to transgress the fourteenth amendment's equal protection clause in their sex-based admissions policy. VMI did not enroll women in their program but created a Virginia Women's Institute for Leadership. The Women's Institute, according to Ginsburg, was not equal to VMI. Justice Ginsburg maintained that VMI failed to show "exceedingly persuasive justification" for such a policy. Justice Antonin Scalia dissented, indicating that the policy's justification was found in the "important governmental interest" of VMI. At the time, VMI was quite a rough program. In her opinion, Justice Ginsburg admitted,

> VMI produces its "citizen soldiers" through "an adversative, or doubting, model of education" which features "[p]hysical rigor, mental stress, absolute equality of treatment, absence of privacy, minute regulation of behavior, and indoctrination in desirable values." As one Commandant of Cadets described it, the adversative method "dissects the young student," and makes him aware of his "limits and capabilities,"

so that he knows "how far he can go with his anger, . . how much he can take under stress, ... exactly what he can do when he is physically exhausted."

VMI cadets live in spartan barracks where surveillance is constant and privacy nonexistent; they wear uniforms, eat together in the mess hall, and regularly participate in drills. Entering students are incessantly exposed to the rat line, "an extreme form of the adversative model," comparable in intensity to Marine Corps boot camp. Tormenting and punishing, the rat line bonds new cadets to their fellow sufferers and, when they have completed the 7 month experience, to their former tormentors.[4]

God tells us that woman is the glory of man (1 Corinthians 11:7). In such a program, one might find an exceedingly persuasive justification for the institute not to enroll "the glory of man." But such a doctrinal justification, nor Justice Scalia's governmental objective justification, nor even a natural revelation justification was sufficient for Justice Ginsburg.

Women's desire and personal ability carried greater weight than the self-evident unsuitableness of the program for the fairer sex. Ginsburg remarked,

> The District Court even allowed that some women *may prefer* [the VMI method] to the methodology a women's college might pursue. "[S]ome women, at least, *would want to* attend [VMI] if they had the opportunity," the District Court recognized, and "some women," the expert testimony established, "*are capable of* all of the individual activities required of VMI cadets...

4 United States v. Virginia et al. (94-1941), 518 U.S. 515 (1996).

the question is whether the State can constitutionally deny to women who have *the will and capacity*,
the training and attendant opportunities that VMI
uniquely affords (emphasis ours).[5]

The false hope of universal equality results in men "tormenting and punishing" women and women wanting to rule
men. This set up is the very curse that came in the wake of our
rebellion against God in the Garden of Eden. God warned us
of what was to come, "To the woman he said ... your desire
shall be contrary to your husband, but he shall rule over you"
(Genesis 3:16).

A FALSE HOPE THAT SUBVERTS THE GOSPEL

The message of autonomy and universal equality is a false
gospel. Salvation concerns overcoming everything that
stands in the way of your being able to express your autonomous self. But, the Bible says salvation is being reconciled
to your Creator. You cannot accomplish that reconciliation
because you have rebelled against Him. Your rebellion has
left you separated and unable to make amends. You need
a redeemer. You need what only God can provide. He has
provided His Son, Jesus Christ. Without His obedient life,
death on the cross, and resurrection, there is no salvation.
Without your being joined to Him through faith, there is no
personal application of His saving work to you.

That saving message cannot be accepted by a person who
continues to adhere to the false hope of equality and autonomy. In the Christian system, you must be reconciled to
God. But from the vantage point of autonomy, you do not

5 Ibid.

need to be reconciled to anything. Nothing outside of the autonomous self is relevant at all. All that matters is your will, ability, and purpose. Likewise, according to universal equality, we all must have exactly the same thing. But the Christian message requires that humanity not have the same thing. There will be sheep and goats, eternal life and eternal death, fellowship with Christ and the outer darkness. And God will have mercy on whom He will have mercy (Romans 9:15).

The Fruitfulness of Christianity

When we know God savingly through His Son, we are freed from sin to live as Christ intends. We leave off the false promises of secularism and take God at His Word. That kind of life, unlike the self-centered and stunted life of unbelief, is fruitful. When man and woman live as God commands, we work for Him together, joyfully sowing and reaping.

When it comes to equality, you can get nothing better than man and woman being created in the image of God. Subjectivity and personal desire do not ground and inform our conception of equality. Instead, the unchanging God Himself grounds and informs how we live as God's image-bearers. In the secular system, equality is tentative and must be relentlessly pursued.

When men and women turn away from self-sufficiency and depend upon God in heaven, then they live well. The woman in Proverbs 31 is a shining example of a godly woman, and she is anything but autonomous. First and foremost, she "fears the Lord" (Proverbs 31:30). Her life's course is directed by God and nurtures others. Her husband has no lack of gain from her (Proverbs 31:11). She feeds her household, and her maidens, too (Proverbs 31:15). The poor find her generosity (Proverbs 31:20). The elders of the land are impacted by her work (Proverbs 31:23). Her children call her blessed (Proverbs 31:28). Many benefit from her teaching and wisdom (Proverbs 31:26). This God-fearing woman does not hope in vain. She is not a lonely, autonomous woman. Her hands are full of fruit (Proverbs 31:31).

ONE GOD, ONE GOSPEL

In the wake of Justice Ginsburg's death, many Americans have been declaring that this is war. They are afraid Roe v. Wade may be overturned. They fear all is lost. Given the false hope of universal equality and autonomy, you can understand the despair that has risen in people. Many people advocate packing the Supreme Court. Others are calling for more riots, saying, "Burn it all down." Why are people responding in these ways? Beneath the surface lies a full-fledged and erroneous faith commitment, one that holds to a vain hope. Their god is under attack.

Our message to all who feel that their god is being assaulted is: There is one God. His name is Yahweh. He is the Creator of all that has been made. He is the only one who is self-sufficient. He is the only one who is self-existent. We are not God. We have sinned, rebelled against God Almighty who has given us everything we have.

John Lenon was wrong. Hell is below us. Heaven is above us. The only way to be saved from eternal death is through Jesus Christ. Jesus is the Son of God made flesh. He is righteous, died on the cross, and rose again. Trust Him and live.

You cannot order your life in such a way, or work a plan so that you will be accepted by God. The only way to be saved is by crying out to the living God, to the Lord Jesus Christ. He saves sinners.

> Amazing grace
> How sweet the sound
> That saved a wretch like me
> I once was lost
> But now am found
> Was blind, but now I see

2

DEFY TYRANTS:
THE LEADERSHIP OF
THE NEW RELIGION

We have identified the new religion as involving the creature worship that the apostle Paul refers to in Romans 1. Humans cannot help but worship something. So, even when we attempt to be "secular," we end up turning something into a god. The new religion operates as if humanity is god. Given that deification of humanity, it is self-evident that we have not yet attained that glorious future state of autonomy and universal equality that is held out by the new religion. Anybody can look around and see that we are not yet in that utopian state of happy oneness. We need people to help us usher in that day.

Enter the leadership of the new religion.

There are different offices of leadership in this religion. Every religion has its prophets. They proclaim the message. America's new religion has many pulpits. They have old and new preachers ranging from Karl Marx and Charles Darwin, through Herbert Marcuse and Peggy McIntosh, to Ta-Nehisi Coates and CNN. The new religion also has many priests.

Priests serve to reconcile the sinner to the religion's god. Planned Parenthood is one of the priests of the new religion. If you stand with them, as they offer the sacrifices, then you will be washed clean and reconciled to the new religion's false god. But the new faith has kings, too. It copies the three offices of the true religion: prophet, priest, and king. The kings use civil authority to enforce the laws of the new religion. They protect the new religion from its enemies. Their goal is to see the false hope of the new religion come to pass.

The kings of the new religion cannot help but be tyrants. They are tyrants because they rebel against the King of Kings under whom they serve. Christians must defy tyrants out of allegiance to King Jesus. We need to grow in our ability to see the overreach of civil authority for what it is: rebellion against Jesus.

TYRANNY IN NEVADA

Governor Steve Sisolak of Nevada engaged in tyrannical government during the COVID pandemic. In the summer of 2020 he ordered the churches in Nevada not to exceed fifty persons when they assemble. At the same time, he permitted casinos, bars, gyms, and other assemblies to meet at 50 percent capacity. Calvary Chapel Dayton Valley applied for injunctive relief. The Supreme Court of the United States denied the church's request. The church's lawyers stated the case plainly:

> If the governor deems it acceptable for secular assemblies to occur at 50 percent capacity at casinos, restaurants, bars, gyms and fitness facilities, indoor and outdoor theme parks, bowling alleys, water

parks, pools, arcades and more, he must apply the same 50 percent capacity rule to constitutionally protected worship services.[1]

Justice Alito wrote a dissenting opinion, and Justices Thomas and Kavanaugh joined him. His words demonstrate that not only did Governor Sisolak rule tyrannically, but the majority of the Supreme Court followed suit:

> The Constitution guarantees the free exercise of religion. It says nothing about the freedom to play craps or blackjack, to feed tokens into a slot machine, or to engage in any other game of chance. But the Governor of Nevada apparently has different priorities. Claiming virtually unbounded power to restrict constitutional rights during the COVID-19 pandemic, he has issued a directive that severely limits attendance at religious services. A church, synagogue, or mosque, regardless of its size, may not admit more than 50 persons, but casinos and certain other favored facilities may admit 50% of their maximum occupancy— and in the case of gigantic Las Vegas casinos, this means that thousands of patrons are allowed.
>
> That Nevada would discriminate in favor of the powerful gaming industry and its employees may not come as a surprise, but this Court's willingness to allow such discrimination is disappointing. We have a duty to defend the Constitution, and even a public health emergency does not absolve us of that responsibility.[2]

---

1 Adam Liptak, "Split 5 to 4, Supreme Court Rejects Nevada Church's Challenge to Shutdown Restrictions," *The New York Times*, July 24, 2020, https://www.nytimes.com/2020/07/24/us/supreme-court-nevada-church-coronavirus.html.

2 *Calvary Chapel Dayton Valley v. Steve Sisolak, Governor of Nevada, et al.*, 591 U.S. 1, 1 (2020) (Alito, dissenting opinion).

Praise God for Justice Alito's dissent. He refers to the first amendment. That amendment does not grant freedom of religion but assures and recognizes that churches will be defended from government oppression. This is an inalienable right granted by the true God to his image-bearers.

Civil authorities must protect life. If a building is on fire or there is an active shooter, they have the authority to disband worship assemblies. But they do not have the authority to prohibit churches without reason or use unequal weights and measures in mandating their COVID restrictions.

We would like to know why Governor Sisolak's great concern for the citizens of the State of Nevada only extends to Christ's Church and not Caesar's Palace? He has been duplicitous and operated outside of his lane. The very authority he wields has been given to him by God above. He is not permitted to use that power to prohibit God's church from assembling. He is also in violation of the United States Constitution, which he swore to uphold when he took office. He attempts to make citizens disobey that Constitution, the highest civil authority in our land. Christians in America who defy governors like Steve Sisolak when they issue illegitimate orders do so in complete agreement with the highest civil authority and God's Word in Roman 13.

Some have pointed out that a church like Calvary Chapel Dayton Valley could comply with Governor Sisolak's order without sinning. They could divide into many smaller churches consisting of less than fifty people. Such a recommendation is not an immediate and clear solution. For example, it is not clear at all that such a decision would be most loving to the tyrant. If one of God's servants uses the sword given him by God to punish the righteous rather than the wicked, do we serve that magistrate well by complying with unlawful dictates?

In the summer of 1651 three Baptists from Rhode Island traveled to Lynn, Massachusetts to hold worship services in the home of an elderly Baptist man. Civil authorities broke into the house and disrupted their worship, arresting John Clarke, John Crandall and Obadiah Holmes for worshiping against the law. Stiff fines were levied against them. Clarke's and Crandall's were paid, but Holmes refused to have his paid and chose instead to endure thirty lashes with a "three-corded whip" on Market Street in downtown Boston. On July 31, 1651, when the sentence was handed down, Holmes stated, "I bless God I am counted worthy to suffer for the name of Jesus." His wounds were so severe that for weeks he had to sleep on his elbows and knees.

Why did Holmes do this? Because he firmly believed that the state had no authority over a man's conscience in dictating to him how he could worship. And he was willing to suffer rather than to give any indication, by paying the fine, that they were correct. News of the beating spread throughout the colonies and around the world, stirring Baptists and others to call for religious liberty in the face of religious persecution. By his resistance, Obadiah Holmes actually helped civil magistrates to serve God better by encouraging them to cease infringing on the religious freedom of citizens in their realm.

Had Calvary Chapel merely acquiesced to Governor Sisolak's overreach they would have missed an opportunity to instruct him and other civil authorities about their responsibilities to honor the God who established them in their office. Further, it is also far from clear that simply complying with his edict by breaking into smaller churches would have been best for the members of that fellowship. How would those new and smaller churches be cared for? Were there enough qualified men to shepherd them?

Neither is it evident that such a decision would have been best for the public witness of the church. If a church obeys this particular unlawful order, how many others will they obey? When will they stop following unlawful orders?

Scripture and history teach us that there is a time to flee persecution. But there is also a time to set our faces toward Jerusalem. There is a time to stand before kings and speak the truth in love. We admit there are gray areas. Each church must determine by God's wisdom how to navigate tough decisions. We will have to choose our battles. But as we do, we must keep in mind that obedience to Jesus Christ will at times necessarily require disobedience to others.

Some have argued that now is not the time for the church to stand up against governmental encroachment. They see the potential challenges coming down the road on the matter of religious freedom and its relationship to the LGBT agenda. The argument claims that we have some big battles to fight then, so we ought not to spend our credibility now on these COVID restriction fights.

The problem with that frame is that it does not understand the times in which we live. The question is not, "Should we stand up now because tougher issues are coming down the road?" Instead, it is, "Why in the world have we not yet stood up, seeing the abominations that have been occurring for some time?" Our educational system has been gutted of any reference to the God of the Bible. The nation protects the fabricated right to murder children. The Obergefell decision now guards the fabricated freedom for people to sin in ways that are against nature itself while calling it marriage. Men have begun to compete against women in athletics, taking their medals. Many more examples could be supplied.

But, in the face of tyrannical rule which has sanctioned these immoral practices, should the church really look to the future and say, "Do not engage yet, because more trouble may come?"

TYRANNY IN CALIFORNIA

Nevada was not the only place that suffered tyranny throughout the COVID pandemic. Governor Gavin Newsom imposed similar restrictions upon churches in California. Pastor John MacArthur and the elders of Grace Church exemplified courage in the face of Newsom's overreach. After weeks of trying to understand the nature and seriousness of the virus as well as the civil authorities' response to it, the church began meeting again. In a public statement entitled, "Christ, Not Caesar, Is Head of the Church," the elders stated,

> Christ is Lord of all. He is the one true head of the church (Ephesians 1:22; 5:23; Colossians 1:18). He is also King of kings—sovereign over every earthly authority (1 Timothy 6:15; Revelation 17:14; 19:16). Grace Community Church has always stood immovably on those biblical principles. As His people, we are subject to His will and commands as revealed in Scripture. Therefore we cannot and will not acquiesce to a government-imposed moratorium on our weekly congregational worship or other regular corporate gatherings. Compliance would be disobedience to our Lord's clear commands.[3]

---

3 "Christ, not Caesar, Is Head of the Church," Grace Church, last modified December 11, 2020, https://www.gracechurch.org/news/posts/1988.

Grace Church understood that the right to assemble is not granted by the government. Jesus is the King, and Jesus does not prohibit meeting in groups for worship. He has commanded that we meet in groups for worship. If civil authorities require that Christians not assemble, then they must justify that prohibition. At the time of Governor Newsom's restrictions, the CDC had listed COVID deaths as only slightly higher than annual flu deaths from previous years. There were simply no grounds for Newsom's church-restricting orders.

Pastors must lead the way in defying tyrants. It is not loving to leave your post. A man is not gracious if he hands over the responsibility Christ gave him to someone whom Christ has not approved. The leadership of Grace Church saw what was at stake:

> As pastors and elders, we cannot hand over to earthly authorities any privilege or power that belongs solely to Christ as head of His church. Pastors and elders are the ones to whom Christ has given the duty and the right to exercise His spiritual authority in the church (1 Peter 5:1–4; Hebrews 13:7, 17).... They have no duty to follow orders from a civil government attempting to regulate the worship or governance of the church. In fact, pastors who cede their Christ-delegated authority in the church to a civil ruler have abdicated their responsibility before their Lord and violated the God-ordained spheres of authority as much as the secular official who illegitimately imposes his authority upon the church.[4]

---

4 Ibid.

Grace Church has provided an example of how to defy tyrants to Christians throughout America. They did so respectfully and based upon God's revealed Word. While many Christian leaders assumed that the loving thing to do was not to assemble the church for worship until civil authority permitted such a gathering, Grace Church demonstrated the necessity of public assembly for the worship of the Creator.

As Christians follow Jesus amid the rise of America's new religion, we must avoid multiple dangers when it comes to civil authorities. We ought not to shake our fist in disrespect at authorities that God has established. On the other hand, our default cannot be to believe everything our governmental authorities tell us. We have good reason not to. Abortion in our land testifies that our government runs roughshod over the sixth commandment. Why should we assume they are going to keep the ninth and tell us the truth? The apostle Peter gives us what we need so that we would avoid both dangers, "Fear God. Honor the emperor" (1 Peter 2:17).

Nero was a wicked ruler. He is often cited where conversations about civil disobedience arise. If the early church was to honor Nero, should we not honor our authorities who are not as evil as him? So the argument goes. One of the breakdowns in that line of reasoning is that many of our modern American authorities make Nero look like a saint. Sixty million babies have been legally murdered in our nation since 1973. Stop and think about that number for a minute. We respectfully ask our pro-choice leaders, "With all of the slaughtered children, are we to believe that your mask mandate has in mind the safety of Americans?" People can take whatever precautions they would like to with the COVID virus. As they do, it seems imminently reasonable to us that they maintain a healthy level of suspicion that pro-choice authorities really care for the well-being of their constituents.

How to Defy Tyrants

We have only considered a couple of examples of the leadership of the new religion. We could fill an entire book with illustrations of tyrannical government in modern-day America. But we would still be left in need of instruction on how to defy such tyranny. By and large, Christians in America lack many of the resources necessary to stand against tyranny. We are confused about God's law; thus, we do not know when it is infringed. We are muddled on the nature and function of love, so we are duped into thinking defying tyrants is uncharitable. We lack warm regard for our country, having bought the lie that we are a terrible nation and have been so from the beginning. In general, we simply lack the courage and faith necessary to suffer the cost of defying tyrants.

Matters of Divine Law

Certain Christian leaders questioned John MacArthur and Grace Church's decision to meet in defiance of Governor Newsom's order. They framed the matter as an issue of Christian liberty. But Christian liberty does not pertain to matters of righteousness and sin. We need to be clear and not confuse those categories. Christian liberty has to do with *adiaphora*, or, indifferent things—it is concerned about matters that God has neither commanded nor forbidden. For example, you can eat meat or not. But whether a church should gather on the Lord's Day to worship is not a matter of Christian liberty. If Christians are not clear on God's law, they will reckon many things as Christian liberty that are, in truth, matters of sin and righteousness.

Likewise, if Christians are not clear on God's law, they will not identify when a civil magistrate encroaches upon God's law. But, of course, you are only to defy tyrants when God's law requires. As indicated before, Christians do not need to point to a particular verse being transgressed in order lawfully to reject a governmental mandate. It is not as if John MacArthur had to find a Bible verse that said, "Thou shalt meet inside when you worship the Almighty" to justify doing so. The elders of Grace Church reasoned from Scripture when they concluded,

> When officials restrict church attendance to a certain number, they attempt to impose a restriction that *in principle* makes it impossible for the saints to gather *as the church*. When officials prohibit singing in worship services, they attempt to impose a restriction that *in principle* makes it impossible for the people of God to obey the commands of Ephesians 5:19 and Colossians 3:16. When officials mandate distancing, they attempt to impose a restriction that *in principle* makes it impossible to experience the close communion between believers that is commanded in Romans 16:16, 1 Corinthians 16:20, 2 Corinthians 13:12, and 1 Thessalonians 5:26. In all those spheres, we must submit to our Lord.[5]

These church leaders reasoned biblically. They considered what God had revealed in His law and determined that the mandate prohibited those things in principle.

---

5 Ibid.

Evangelism and Public Witness

Confusion over evangelism and public witness creates difficulties for standing against tyranny. Paul set a glorious example as he became all things to all people that he might save some (1 Corinthians 9:22). But there are qualifications to that principle. Paul did not engage in sin so that sinners might come to Jesus Christ. He did not worship Caesar so that Romans would bow the knee to Jesus Christ. Modern approaches to evangelism have misconstrued this Pauline principle, thinking that evangelism's first goal is to be liked. Upon being accepted as a likable individual, you can then proceed to speak the gospel so that your listener might hear and believe. Such an approach is marked by pragmatic unbelief rather than hope in the sovereign God who saves sinners.

The public witness of God's people has very often occurred in conjunction with their defying of tyrants. Such was the case in Moses' day. Pharaoh oppressed God's people, and Moses confronted him in the power of God. The same occurred with Mordecai and Haman. The result was the glory of God in the judgment of the wicked and salvation of His people. Christ Himself publicly testified the truth concerning Himself, and in so doing, defied the civil rulers of His day. The apostles did the same in Jerusalem, obeying God rather than the Jewish authorities who told them to stop preaching. Paul followed suit as He took the gospel of Jesus Christ from town to town, often suffering at the hands of authorities.

Paul preached the gospel in such a way in the city of Thessalonica that a riot ensued (Acts 17:1-9). Civil authorities got involved, and Paul had to flee the city. One can imagine how many American evangelical leaders would have responded to the apostle, "Paul, you must learn to be more charitable. We will never keep up a good reputation in the city of Thessalonica if you keep stirring the city up into an uproar. Think about the new believers at the recent church plant. How hard it will be for them to follow Christ now."

Admittedly, many American Christians are trying to catch up with the shift that has taken place in their midst. Not long ago, believers were generally accepted by the culture. People had some respect for Christians even if they did not confess the faith once for all delivered to the saints. But things have changed. Believers must now work through false charges. They have not had a great deal of experience with being told that they have done something immoral when, in truth, they have not. The tendency can be to either stay away and not go out into the world to speak for Christ or to play down the parts of Christian truth that are not in harmony with the spirit of the day. Both roads are wrong. Rather, we should entrust ourselves to our sovereign God and speak the truth in love. In standing against tyranny, we actually have an incredible opportunity to point people to the true King whose yoke is easy and burden light.

LOVE OF NEIGHBOR

You will have all sorts of trouble defying tyrants if you are confused about love. Secularism has attempted to change the dictionary so that love is essentially accepting someone for who they are. But God is the one who defines love. Jesus was pretty loving, and He got crucified. People hated Him. But the evangelical mind says that if people hate you, then you must not be loving. You certainly could have been more charitable. "What did you expect?" they say, "You disobeyed your civil authorities. Your witness is now shot." But genuine love "does not rejoice at wrongdoing, but rejoices with the truth" (1 Corinthians 13:6). If civil authorities mandate wrongdoing, then to defy them is love to neighbor. We have heard many Christian leaders say something like, "We decided that the most loving thing we could do was wear a mask. We decided just to love our neighbor during this season and not meet." Our response has been, "We decided to love our neighbor and assemble the church." What could be more loving to neighbors than to keep up the public worship of the God who gives life to all people?

Defying tyrants is not only a way to love fellow citizens. It is actually a way to love the tyrants themselves. Anytime people with authority abuse that authority, a loving person would tell them. How much do you have to hate someone to let him go on ruling as a tyrant? Many Christians across America have objected to various kinds of arbitrary civil orders. Pastors have been fined. Christians have been threatened, and some arrested. If we are not careful, we can think that those who object are the "defying tyrants kind of Christians" and those who comply are the "peace-loving, gentle, humble, and gracious-kind-of-Christians." But that set up is wrong-headed. Those believers who have respectfully and humbly protested injustices from civil magistrates have been the ones who have loved. We cannot say that those who have remained silent about criminal overreach from governmental authorities have been loving. They have been silent. But that is an altogether different thing than being loving.

We need a fresh understanding of the cost of love. Jesus said, "Greater love has no one than this, that someone lay down his life for his friends" (John 15:13). By God's grace, we are not yet at the point where martyrdom is a common experience in the Christian West. But our brothers and sisters from around the globe have reminded us many times that their persecution has made them strong, and our prosperity has made us weak. Genuine love for neighbor will be sacrificial. When we defy tyrants, there will be a price to pay. We should prepare ourselves to lose our resources, our incomes, our buildings, and more. Such losses shall come in the pursuit of our neighbor's welfare.

Along with the love of neighbor and governing authorities, defying tyrants involves the love of country. Our nation has been blessed of God in many ways. In its founding and for much of its history, our nation has recognized that there is a God in heaven. America has acknowledged, not adequately enough at times, that God endowed His image-bearers with inalienable rights. The country certainly has not always lived up to that ideal. The abominable slave trade is a glaring example. The holocaust of abortion is the modern-day indictment. But it was that very pre-commitment to the image of God in man that eventually led to the end of slavery.

Those who would abide tyranny must be asked, "Do you love your country?" The deconstructive forces that have been unleashed on our nation have an agenda. They have a goal to completely overthrow and pull down what has been good and blessed of God in this nation. Again, America has all kinds of paganism in it; it is godless in many ways. But many have lived and prospered in this nation. And there is a heritage of Judeo-Christian thought and principle that still speaks today if we take time to listen. From the shores of this country the gospel has sounded forth around the world. Ours is a nation worth standing up for. So we must resist governmental oppression. We must defy tyrants. We resolve to proclaim the kingship of Jesus over every square inch of this nation and His world, which He created.

HERE WE STAND

Under the providence of God, we have no reason to panic. We have no reason to despair. But we ought to discern the times. Our assessment is that it is time for Christians and churches to humble themselves, repent, and call upon God to come and act. We are not getting out of the mess we are in apart from God's almighty power. As we look to Him, we must stand uncompromisingly on His truth. Paul would not give an inch to those who twisted true religion. So, too, we must not give an inch to those who would advance a false religion.

What you do right now matters. Our Christian fathers and mothers have suffered much at the hand of tyrants. They were falsely accused of all sorts of immorality. Godless authorities tried to manipulate them and paint them as rebels and even cannibals. Now, for the first time in a long time, the American church has the opportunity to take their place and suffer for the Name. As Spurgeon once said, "Here is the day for the man, where is the man for the day?"[6]

Fear God. Defy tyrants.

---

6 Charles Spurgeon, "Holding Fast the Faith," Sermon preached on February 5, 1888.

3

RESIST ANARCHY:
THE SPIRIT OF THE NEW RELIGION

In the new religion, man is god, the human will is the holy standard, and human desire is unrestrained. We have seen the false gospel of this twisted faith. It maintains that a great kingdom is coming to pass, but it is not Christ's kingdom. Instead, it is the kingdom of universal equality and autonomy, in which we will one day happily live as one with no possessions, no heaven or hell, and nothing to live or die for. The leadership of the new religion cracks the whip so that the glorious day might come to fruition. Like the enslaver Pharaoh, they rule harshly over mankind, disregarding God's clear instructions to them. These tyrants must be defied. But defying tyrants has nothing to do with giving in to the spirit of anarchy. Indeed, defying tyrants is what law-abiding people do. Supporting tyrants is what anarchists do.

Anarchy is the spirit of the new religion. Having rejected God, the secularist has no ultimate standard to which he might appeal. Even so, as secularism hardens, rules and regulations come with it. But they are not just rules. They are not standards that have some reference to a higher law. They are merely expressions of the human will. America finds itself in a very similar situation to Israel during the time of the judges, "In those days there was no king in Israel. Everyone did what was right in his own eyes" (Judges 21:25). That line is the definition of anarchy: "absence of government; a state of lawlessness due to the absence or inefficiency of the supreme power; political disorder."[7]

The spirit of anarchy has found fresh wind and presently pulsates in America. We happen to be writing this chapter on the morning of the United States presidential election. The year 2020 has not been a typical election year. For the first time we can remember, cities across the nation are preparing for rioting and looting in the wake of election day:

> It's an eerie sight in a country built on the idea of a peaceful transition of power. In fact, that kind of signal is exactly why city authorities have generally advised business owners not to board up, promising stepped-up security measures. Still, plywood panels are dotting major streets in Boston and New York, San Francisco and Los Angeles, Chicago and Washington, D.C. Store owners are on edge from breakins during the summer.[8]

An Opportunity to Wake Up

People need to wake up to the spirit of anarchy, understanding it in light of the new religion. Some Christian leaders have

---

7 OED Online, s.v. "anarchy," accessed November 3, 2020, https://www.oed.com/view/Entry/7118.

8 Alina Selyukh, "A Sign of the Times: Across U.S., City Storefronts Boarded Up Ahead of Election," NPR, November 2, 2020. https://www.npr.org/2020/11/02/930371341/an-abundance-of-caution-across-u-s-city-storefronts-boarded-up-ahead-of-election.

spoken out against the riots. But, regrettably, many Christian leaders have failed to renounce the riots. Shockingly, some have nearly justified the anarchy. In general, Christians in America have not stood with a clear voice and resisted the spirit of lawlessness growing in our nation. Such a failure is shocking, in part, because you do not have to be a Christian to see the folly of rioting. It is against nature.

The apostle Paul was once in Ephesus. Due to his gospel preaching, some were enraged, and the city was filled with confusion. The people rushed together, and the unrest grew. Amid the yelling and chanting, we hear of a town clerk who warned the crowd that they were in danger of being charged with rioting (Acts 19:40).

It is insightful to see that the rioting was fueled by a devotion to false gods and personal gain. Paul's preaching was turning people away from the worship of the goddess Artemis. Many Ephesians were devoted to her and did not like the change. The craftsmen were also losing their work because people were no longer buying their silver shrines of Artemis. Moderns may look back and think that the ruckus was all about the money. But the truth is the rioting was all about both the false worship and the money. The same is true in America today. However troubling things were in Ephesus, the town clerk had the wherewithal to tell them to knock it off. The people listened and were dismissed (Acts 19:41).

Thank God for a town-clerk-like situation that came up with one Tennessee State Representative. He is a pro-life democrat. While we have major problems with the Democrat Party platform, it is remarkable and indicting that this representative has spoken with more courage than many of our evangelical leaders. While in session, he stood to say the following to his colleagues:

If we don't start standing for something, don't you know that the people who are looking at what's happening in Washington, in Detroit, in Portland and Seattle, they are getting emboldened because we act like a bunch of punks, too frightened to stand up and protect our own stuff? You tell me that somebody has got the right to tear down property that Tennessee taxpayers paid for, that American taxpayers paid for, and somebody has the right to destroy it, deface it, and tear it down? What kind of people have we become that we can't protect our own stuff? Peaceful protest ends peacefully. Anarchy ends in chaos.[9]

While this Representative, John Deberry, exemplifies the courage to face up to the riots, many have tried to diminish and distract from the spirit of anarchy. Some have said that people are merely expressing themselves, and we need to listen. CNN actually released footage of burning buildings with the caption, "Fiery But Mostly Peaceful Protests After Police Shooting."[10] We should not be surprised by these things. Humanity is in the business of concealing sin. We do not want to take responsibility. We do not want to confess. But, as the Puritans said, the way down is the way up. We will not get out of the mess we are in if we do not come to grips with our rebellion against God. The burning buildings afford us an opportunity to see that we hate the Great Judge.

9　Zachary Evans, "'We Act Like a Bunch of Punks:' Black Tennessee Lawmaker Shames Rioters, Invokes Family Legacy of Peaceful Protest," *National Review*, August 28, 2020, https://www.nationalreview.com/news/we-act-like-a-bunch-of-punks-black-tennessee-lawmaker-shames-rioters-invokes-family-legacy-of-peaceful-protest.

10　Joe Concha, "CNN ridiculed for 'Fiery But Mostly Peaceful' caption with video of burning building in Kenosha," The Hill, August 27, 2020, https://thehill.com/homenews/media/513902-cnn-ridiculed-for-fiery-but-mostly-peaceful-caption-with-video-of-burning.

ANARCHY: THE FRUIT OF THE FALSE RELIGION

We make no predictions about what will come in American life in the months and years to come. But we do object to the notion that our civil unrest is normal, run-of-the-mill election year happenings. Some may think that everything will be fine if we simply get through the election and get the right man in office. Indeed, we see the benefit of having the conservative-judge-appointing man win, rather than the kill-the-babies candidate. Even so, our social problems spring from problems down below. We observe the budding of some very bad ideologies that have been with us for far too long. Our social upheaval has been manufactured. People are pulling strings. We need the moral fortitude to stop it.

The process begins with rejecting God and ends up in boarding up New York City on Election Day. When you reject the Creator, you will still worship something. In one way or another, you exalt the creation. We have been doing that for some time. We consider ourselves the gods of our own universe. We have made great strides in science. But, rather than thinking of those discoveries as gifts from God, who has enabled us to understand His world, we see them as man's conquest over nature. We have learned how to press a button and get a certain outcome, forgetting that God is the One who made the button and the outcome. We have also neglected that He made our finger and maintains the relationship between the button and the outcome.

The discerning people of the human race, having forgotten God, can still see the cause and effect dynamic of our world. We have disregarded the manual. We have ignored the Designer. But we have a basic understanding of the lights and the switches. In short, we see that pitching a fit in Walmart can often get us a candy bar. When we get older, we discover that setting fire to storefronts can be a lucrative endeavor. This behavior is especially the case when society has lost its backbone and cannot resist anarchy.

A materialistic and mechanistic worldview has set in upon us. We see it on both the right and the left. The left, in general, constitutes the fire starters. They press the button in anticipation of the reward. But many on the right are given to this same worldview. They have become pragmatic to the point that they no longer look to the heavens. So you may get one of two responses from them when the left throws a tantrum. They might, in the first place, decide to double the recipe and return like for like. They know how the game is played. So they come back with greater force. On the other hand, they may soothe the fitful child with some sort of candy, even if it is not the desired and very costly one. The first response is the child-abuser who responds to the fit with hostility. The second is the child-enabler, who gives in as a way to get the groceries in peace.

Both options fail to look to an ultimate standard and resist the spirit of anarchy. The former teaches the child that he can exasperate mom. The latter teaches the child that he can manipulate mom. Our social dynamic between right and left is, in essence, a materialistic mom trying to keep a materialistic child under control. They both operate out of a mechanistic worldview, ignoring the God in heaven who has spoken.

GOD RULES OVER THE REBELS

But, the spirit of anarchy does more than simply ignore God. It rebels against Him. This rebellion is marked in Psalm 2,

"Why do the nations rage and the peoples plot in vain? The kings of the earth set themselves, and the rulers take counsel together, against the LORD and against his Anointed, saying, 'Let us burst their bonds apart and cast away their cords from us'" (Psalm 2:1-2). Fallen man believes that God's rule is a shackle that must be broken. Yet they have no reason for their rebellion. The psalmist rightly asks, "Why do the nations rage?" But no answer can be given. You cannot find a just cause. Even so, their rebellion is strategic. They plot and scheme against the Lord. Their agenda, however, is doomed to fail. Their rebellion is vain. The One against whom they rebel is the Creator Himself.

What is He doing? Laughing. It is not a happy laugh; it is a laugh of mockery—"The Lord holds them in derision" (Psalm 2:4). He ridicules them. His mocking laugh serves as a preamble to His terrifying Word to them, "Then he will speak to them in his wrath" (Psalm 2:5). Judgment and salvation both come from the Father as He appoints His Son to rule the nations. Those anarchic nations will become His heritage; the very ends of the earth will be His possession (Psalm 2:8). The spirit that drives the new religion will be squelched either way. Individuals will either "kiss the Son," or they will be broken with "a rod of iron" (Psalm 2:12, 9).

Psalm 2 teaches that God rules over the rebels. Christians need not try to rule over rebels the way God does. Instead, we can resist anarchy by faith in the Son. We follow the psalmist who did not run and hide from raging people or justify their rioting. Instead, he testified the truth amid their tumult, "Now therefore, O kings, be wise; be warned, O rulers of the earth. Serve the LORD with fear, and rejoice with trembling" (Psalm 2:10-11). Faith in the God who laughs at rebellion fuels courage to resist anarchy.

RESISTANCE: THE RIGHT RESPONSE TO ANARCHY

Christians must be witnesses to God's standard. They say, "There is a standard here, and I am not going to budge." By word and deed, we point to God and His rule.

In times of civil unrest, it is that much more important for Christians to think through their responsibility to protect life. Wisdom is required to determine when force is legitimate, and when it is not. The sixth commandment says, "You shall not murder." That command prohibits taking life, but it also requires protecting life. Question 73 of the Baptist Catechism states:

> Q: What is required in the sixth commandment?
>
> A: The sixth commandment requireth all lawful endeavours to preserve our own life (Eph. 5:28, 29) and the life of others (1 Kings 18:4).[11]

Men, particularly, are to be protectors. In times of anarchy, we must not neglect our responsibility to protect life. We should be aware of the laws of our land, the tools with which we might protect life, and the appropriate measures to take in life-threatening situations.

We are not the first to encounter hostile days. Francis Schaeffer has wisely said, "There does come a time when force, even physical force, is appropriate. The Christian is not to take the law into his own hands and become a law unto himself. But when all avenues to flight and protest have closed, force in the defensive posture is appropriate."[12]

---

11 "The Baptist Catechism," Founders Ministries, accessed November 3, 2020, https://founders.org/library/the-baptist-catechism.

12 Francis Schaeffer, *A Christian Manifesto* (Wheaton, IL: Crossway, 1981), 117.

The use of force can get extremely confusing in this mob-like world in which we now live. Civil authorities in certain regions have been very slow if not nearly unable to stop the riots. Believers need to think through their responsibility to protect life in such situations.

RESISTING IDEOLOGIES OF ANARCHY

Along with physical resistance, we must be prepared to resist anarchical ideologies. Our culture has indoctrinated the rising generation to view liberty and law as irreconcilable enemies. Patrick Deneen put it well, "In contrast to ancient theory—which understood liberty to be achieved only through virtuous self-government—modern theory defines liberty as the greatest possible pursuit and satisfaction of the appetites, while government is a conventional and unnatural limitation upon this pursuit."[13] The result of this erroneous notion of liberty is disastrous:

> In this world, gratitude to the past and obligations to the future are replaced by a nearly universal pursuit of immediate gratification: culture, rather than imparting the wisdom and experience of the past so as to cultivate virtues of self-restraint and civility, becomes synonymous with hedonic titillation, visceral crudeness, and distraction, all oriented toward promoting consumption, appetite, and detachment. As a result, superficially self-maximizing, socially destructive behaviors begin to dominate society.[14]

---

13 Patrick Deneen, *Why Liberalism Failed* (New Haven, CT: Yale University Press, 2018), 48.

14 Ibid., 39

We are reaping the fruit of our ideologies. We need not look far to see these socially destructive behaviors that now begin to dominate our society. Evangelical leaders who support, however indirectly, organizations like Black Lives Matter cannot say that they love others. The ideology at the heart of the Black Lives Matter organization is destructive, both physically and spiritually.

Pastors must be willing to shepherd their people through these times. We shepherd people body and soul. We are not imaginary shepherds, caring for people as they navigate their imagination. We preach truth to people so that they can live in the real world by faith. We face new ethical challenges. And life comes at our people at a rapid pace.

Sadly, many pastors have found a way to shepherd in mid-air. They do not help their people follow Jesus through real life. Even within the evangelical world, bad actors seek to sideline pastors with comments like, "In the midst of COVID, remember Pastor, you are not a doctor." To which we reply, "Yes, we are not doctors, but we can count. We can read." The same play is run in different ways, "You are not a military professional, so quiet down about the use of force." Or, "You are not a legal scholar, so what right do you have to address the Supreme Court opinions?" Indeed, every pastor has his limitations. There is a way to get out on the skinny branches. But, all of life is doctrinal. Faith in Christ concerns all of life. And it is that very point which the evangelical church has largely neglected. As Schaeffer has said, "Christianity and spirituality were shut up to a small isolated part of life. The totality of reality was ignored by the pietistic thinking... True spirituality covers all of reality... the Lordship of Christ covers *all* of life and *all* of life equally."[15]

---

15 Francis Schaeffer, *A Christian Manifesto*, 19.

In short, pastor, your people need you to teach them how to resist anarchy.

TEACHING GOD'S LAW TO ANARCHISTS

Every time a looter steals from Target, a fire is set to a business, or someone is brutally attacked, it is a rebellious act against God. Such people have violated the law of their Creator. They have done many other things, too. We are not downplaying the horizontal dimensions of these actions. But, if we fail to see these matters as the transgression of divine law, we will not fulfill our Christian duty.

The church must preach God's law. We are not trying to get justified through obedience to the law. We preach law to help the lost see they are lost. It was, after all, Paul who said,

> What then shall we say? That the law is sin? By no means! Yet if it had not been for the law, I would not have known sin. For I would not have known what it is to covet if the law had not said, "You shall not covet." But sin, seizing an opportunity through the commandment, produced in me all kinds of covetousness. For apart from the law, sin lies dead. I was once alive apart from the law, but when the commandment came, sin came alive and I died. The very commandment that promised life proved to be death to me (Romans 7:7-10).

We preach God's law to help people come to grips with the fact that they have to deal with God. They may only be thinking about civil authorities. But, in reality, their problem is with God. They rebel against Him.

Because of such rebellion, God sent His Son into the world. He was the great resister of anarchy. He was tempted by the chief rebel, Satan. But, Christ submitted His will to the Father. He did not come to abolish the law but perfectly fulfilled the law for wretched anarchists.

Believers in Christ have no room whatsoever to look down our nose at the brick throwers. We do not resist them with a snarl of arrogance. We know them very well. Such were some of us. Indeed, such were all of us. But for the glory of God and the good of humanity, we cannot drag our feet when it comes to heralding the law and gospel of Christ.

REAPING THE WHIRLWIND

Do not let yourself think that the year 2020 was just a hiccup. It has not been a random blip on our radar screen, happening to pop up without reason. Paul says, "Do not be deceived: God is not mocked, for whatever one sows, that will he also reap" (Galatians 6:7). The civil unrest that we have observed is the bubbling over of the spirit that gives life to the new religion. That spirit is a spirit of anarchy that seeks to cast off God and His truth.

Christians should not be surprised that we have to resist such a spirit. James tells us, "Submit yourselves therefore to God. Resist the devil, and he will flee from you" (James 4:7). But, as with all of God's commands, we obey them by grace through faith. Ours is not merely a pragmatic resistance. We resist through prayer, acknowledging God who must help us—"Unless the LORD watches over the city, the watchman stays awake in vain" (Psalm 127:1). We need revival in our churches. We need pastors that have courage and backbone. We need police officers who fear God. We need political leaders that operate according to the constitution and are held accountable by a faithful Christian witness.

Our resistance must start at ground zero. Ground zero is our very own life—"What causes quarrels and what causes fights among you? Is it not this, that your passions are at war within you? You desire and do not have, so you murder. You covet and cannot obtain, so you fight and quarrel" (James 4:1-2). The way for sinners to turn away from rebellion is crystal clear. All one must do is, "Kiss the Son" for "blessed are all who take refuge in him" (Psalm 2:12).

PART 2:

ON THE OFFENSE

4

TAKE RESPONSIBILITY: THE ANTIDOTE TO LAWLESS RIOTS & RACIAL CONFUSION

The barrel was full of gun powder. We had spent several decades filling that particular powder keg. But the tragic death of George Floyd in Minneapolis, Minnesota, lit the fuse. The video of a police officer kneeling on the neck of Floyd circulated throughout the nation. The city of Minneapolis erupted in violence. Looters had their way with local stores. Buildings burned. Riots filled the streets. But mayhem did not limit itself to Minneapolis. All across the country, civil unrest ensued.

The year 2020 has sent us a clear message: America needs a dad. We are childish, arrogant, and afraid. The times call for responsibility and restraint, but those characteristics are in short order. We have become untethered from God and His Word. There is nowhere else for us to go but to the law and the prophets. In divine truth, we find what we need to sort out the mess on our hands. In the light of revelation, we can understand what is taking place in all of these things: the disturbing death of George Floyd, the aftermath of anarchy, and the irresponsible way our civil and religious leaders have addressed our nation's trouble.

LAWLESSNESS AND CONFUSION

At the bottom of our society's turmoil is lawlessness. According to God's Word, police officers have God-ordained authority (Romans 13). They have a high calling to wield that authority in responsible ways. Indeed, many citizens do not know what it is like to be in the dangerous situations that law enforcement officers regularly face. Even so, the officers must abide by God's law and execute their duties with appropriate restraint.

Sadly, responsibility did not mark much of the public response to Floyd's death. People believed they could go burn down businesses, trash cities, murder policemen, and destroy their property. What is that? Well, that is lawlessness. Should there be protests and speaking out? Yes. Should there be anger? Absolutely. But there are appropriate ways and lawless ways. What has occurred in America over many months of 2020 is lawless.

Our civil and religious leadership demonstrate confusion in the way they frame our civil trouble. Some want to speak the truth in love but seem only to maintain a superficial knowledge of God's Word. Others lack the courage to say anything and seem to lack concern over the crumbling of our civilization. God's Word, if acknowledged at all, is only given a passing glance. What God says about right and wrong is assumed or sublimated.

It is lawlessness all the way around.

THE PROBLEM OF AUTHORITY

We have a problem with authority in America. We have swallowed the poison pill, which teaches us that hierarchy is bad. Even within conservative Christian circles, there have been calls for the tearing down of all hierarchy. That demolition job is what the sexual revolution has been aiming at for some time. We have failed to understand what Bob Dylan grasped, "You're gonna have to serve somebody."

We do not live in an egalitarian creation. Nature maintains queen bees and kings of the jungle. The military has generals and privates. Your home has lights which obey the will of the power plant through the mediating officer of the light switch. Hierarchy and authority are inescapable because God designed the world along these lines. If you live contrary to God's design, you are living in a dream world. You open yourself to manipulation and abuse of authority. That manipulative abuse is precisely what happened to the comrades on Orwell's *Animal Farm*. They discovered that "all animals are equal, but some animals are more equal than others."[1]

No human has unlimited authority. One way that God has limited human authority is by placing it within certain spheres. He ordained authority to be exercised in the realms of the home, the church, and society. Genesis tells the story of the first husband and wife. God created Adam first, then Eve. Adam is the leader. He names Eve. God went to Adam first when things went wrong. The pre-fall relational arrangement between Adam and Eve was one in which he led, and she helped. After the fall, that relationship was troubled, and it is troubled down to this day. Many husbands will now rule harshly over their wives. Likewise, several wives will be against their husbands. When we were cast out of the Garden, the relational structure itself did not change, but our operation within that structure was deeply troubled.

God established authority in the church, too. He tells Christians, "Obey your leaders and submit to them, for they

---

1 George Orwell, *Animal Farm* (New York, NY: Signet Classics, 1996).

are keeping watch over your souls, as those who will have to give an account" (Hebrews 13:17). So, church leaders do not have unlimited authority. They, too, have an authority to which they report. The congregation itself has authority, as seen in texts like Matthew 18:17 and 1 Corinthians 5:4.

In the civil realm, God has established authority as well. The home maintains the authority of the rod (Proverbs 22:15). The church exercises ecclesiastical authority through discipline (Matthew 18:17). Civil authority wields the sword (1 Peter 2:13-17; Romans 13:1-7).

When you have fallen people leading fallen people, then you are going to have problems with authority. But, an attempt to level the very structure of creation will not help us at all. We must see how God has designed the world to work. Apart from Christ, we will never happily live according to God's design. But, in Christ, we can be restored to submit to and exercise authority as God intends.

RESPONSIBILITY AND RESTRAINT

Responsibility and authority go hand in hand. Where you have an individual taking responsibility, he will soon likely have a measure of authority. On the other hand, if a person with authority fails to take responsibility, very often that authority will eventually be removed from him.

The relationship between responsibility and authority appears in the Garden of Eden. The New Testament clarifies what we already see in the Garden, "the head of every man is Christ, the head of a wife is her husband, and the head of Christ is God" (1 Corinthians 11:3). With that position of authority comes the assumption of responsibility. So even though Eve was the first to eat the fruit, God came to Adam first when His law was transgressed. Why? Because Adam was responsible. The first thing that fallen man does is shirk responsibility. When asked if he had eaten the fruit, Adam replied, "The woman whom you gave to be with me, she gave me the fruit of the tree, and I ate" (Genesis 3:12).

Peculiar challenges come with responsibility. Praise God for our police officers in America. They do dangerous and honorable work. Average citizens do not understand what is involved in policing. Officers must regularly put themselves in positions in which they do not know who has a weapon or what will occur. Such challenges, however, only increase the need for responsibility and restraint.

The fear of God is essential to restraint. If you fear God, then you do not need to fear man. If you do not fear God, then you will fear man. The fear of man results in the loss of restraint. Authorities of any kind will domineer over and micromanage those under their jurisdiction. They will be consumed with worry that things will not turn out well. Such people cannot help but operate out of the fear of man. The God-fearing authority knows that without God, there is no hope. That truth does not result in laziness. Such a leader will work hard and expect those under his or her care to work hard. But the diligent work, done in faith, is full of joy. Authorities who fear God are hopeful that God will work for His glory and their good. They expect God to be God; and they expect those under their care to be human.

Christians ought not to be surprised then when they see abuse of authority. God has told us that all have fallen short, and "there is no fear of God before their eyes" (Romans 3:18). We, however, who have come to the Lord Jesus, can exercise authority well. We can restrain ourselves, not domineering over those in our charge. We can take responsibility for situations that have gone wrong without assuming the guilt of particular sins we did not commit.

ETHNIC GNOSTICISM

As fallen people, we often think we know something is true when, in reality, it is not. We are confident that we are despised by the person who failed to wave back at us. It does not matter that the individual may not have seen us. It is not worth considering if the person was distracted by something that happened to him or her earlier that day. We simply know that we are despised. There is no need to prove it. If you require proof, you are a part of the problem. Everyone knows that if you do not get a wave back, it means the person hates you.

Voddie Bauchum calls this kind of thing, as it applies to relationships between whites and blacks, Ethnic Gnosticism. Gnosticism was a heresy that involved having a special and unmediated knowledge that separated you from others. People of all sexes and skin colors can get caught up in this error. Bauchum explains how the idea not only applies to race but also to modern conceptions of sexuality and transgenderism. According to the new religion, minorities or seemingly oppressed people groups simply know they are being oppressed. They do not need to justify or prove the reality of their oppression. If you are not a minority, then you would not understand anyway.

Many have advanced the Ethnic Gnosticism idea in the wake of George Floyd's death. It is not enough to lament that an image-bearer of God died. The problem is not only with police training, technique, and restraint. The problem, we have been assured by Ethnic Gnostics, is the oppression of minority blacks by majority whites. You do not need any evidence that the police officers involved are racist. You do not need to discover whether they uttered any racist speech or seek to revive the KKK. People simply know that what occurred in George Floyd's death was racist.

Evidence could be brought forth that demonstrates that one or more of the four police officers involved is indeed racist. But that does not disprove the problematic point at hand. The fact is, many people instinctively claimed, before any evidence, that Floyd's death was an example of systemic racial oppression. Such an instinctive claim is natural, given the worldview from which it rises. That worldview is the worldview of Cultural Marxism.[2]

Cultural Marxism is an adaptation of classical Marxism moving it from an economic theory to a cultural and social one. Classical Marxism sees class conflict between the bourgeoisie and the proletariat—or the "haves" and "have-nots." Cultural Marxism extends such conflict beyond economics to include any social relationship that can be defined in terms of those who are oppressed and their oppressors; between those with privilege and those without it. The working class has been replaced by cultural and social minorities. Majority groups are defined as "privileged" and "oppressive." Minority groups are regarded as "underprivileged" and "oppressed."

Through the lens of intersectionality whites, men, heterosexuals, cisgenders, Christians, and the able-bodied are all majority groups and therefore inherently oppressive. They comprise the "dominant culture" and wield "hegemonic power" against sub-dominant cultures. "Hegemony" comes

---

2 Bauchum explains that Ethnic Gnosticism is rooted in Cultural Marxism. Voddie Baucham, *By What Standard? God's World . . . God's Rules* (Cape Coral, FL: Founders Press, 2020), 106.

from a Greek term that means "to have dominance over." It is the word that twentieth-century Italian Marxist, Antonio Gramsci employed to describe the moral, ideological, and cultural dominance that majority groups exert over minorities. Those who do not fit into such majority groups are "sub-dominant" minorities and by definition, in the cultural Marxist scheme, oppressed. Those in the dominant culture exert their hegemonic power over minorities by manipulating them—oftentimes inadvertently—to accept their cultural assumptions, mores and values.

Whatever groups are identified as oppressed, it is vital that the people in that group accept the fact of their oppression. If they do not believe they are oppressed, then as Gramsci postulated, they have bought into the hegemony's worldview, and the revolution cannot take place. Here is where Ethnic Gnosticism comes in. People must know intuitively that certain identities are oppressed. When a particular case arises, it is not sufficient to understand that a wrong occurred. You must know that the wrong was systemic—a privileged class representative oppressed a victim class representative.

This way of viewing the world (Cultural Marxism) has given rise to a philosophical movement or ideology known as Critical Theory (or Critical Social Theory). Critical theory is a theory of social relationships that is not satisfied simply to understand them (as Traditional Social Theory does) but insists on critiquing and deconstructing society as a whole in order to improve it.[3]

Its agenda is to see the overthrow of these oppressive groups and the deconstruction of those structures that enable them

---

3 *Stanford Encyclopedia of Philosophy Archive*, Fall 2016 ed., "Critical Theory." Stanford: Stanford University, 2005. https://plato.stanford.edu/archives/fall2016/entries/critical-theory/ (November 12, 2020).

to wield their hegemonic power—all in the name of love and compassion for the oppressed. The blood-letting that was witnessed on the streets of America in 2020 is nothing less than the fruit of this worldview.

TAKING RESPONSIBILITY

To summarize, lawlessness and confusion run rampant in America. We have a serious problem with authority. Restraint and responsibility have been thrown to the wind. Adherents of the new religion are ferociously driven to gain their neighbor's belongings. Many are so deeply vested in the Cultural Marxist/Critical Theory framework that they claim categorical oppression, which not only does not need to be proven but, indeed, cannot be proven to oppressor classes.

Many people hesitate to take responsibility for correcting the errors which have been mentioned in this chapter. Some hesitancy is understandable. Are you ready to run for the hills? Several want to say, "Not my problem. I'm out of here." Such a sentiment is not an option for followers of Christ. These problems are our problems. We all created this mess when we ate the fruit. God has told us to go make disciples. He has told us to conquer the land, being strong and coura-geous (Joshua 1:6). He has given us His Word. We are not infallible, but God's Word is. We are not ashamed of it. If we let someone go on in an erroneous faith, we cannot say that we love them. Such neglect is hateful. So, what is involved in taking responsibility in the face of lawlessness and confusion?

Set Your House in Order

Jesus was wise when he said to remove the log from your own eye before you help another with his speck (Matthew 7:5).

In many ways, the church has become accustomed to complaining about what is happening out there in the world. We lament it. We guard against it, making sure it does not come into the church. And amen for defensive measures. But, we are the primary failures when it comes to authority and responsibility. We have become comfortable in our private meetings and cut ourselves off from the world in the wrong ways. We have forgotten that Jesus has all authority in heaven and on earth (Matthew 28:18). We have shirked our responsibility to go and teach people to observe Jesus' commandments.

Given the riots, it is easy to shake our heads in disgust at a rioter who throws a Molotov cocktail through a store window. At the highest levels of our civil leadership, we see media posts that exacerbate the situation. We cannot imagine how people could escalate tensions rather than communicate truth, love, and direction. But as we said before, America needs a dad. Christians are the ones who know the Father. We have the Father. Our Father has told us to make Him known from Jerusalem, Judea, unto the ends of the earth.

If we are to teach the world about authority and responsibility, we must ensure we practice both faithfully. We know what it means to fall short. The curse of the fall has touched us all. But we have everything we need in Christ to repent of sin and press on in faith. As we do so, a number of topics need biblical clarity.

Racism

Christians must take responsibility to define racism accurately. Racism is a particular kind of pride and hatred. We can be prideful and hateful without any regard to ethnicity. But when we are arrogant or malicious based on ethnicity, then we have an example of racism. Both of those sins, pride and malice, can appear in various degrees. You can be a little prideful. You can harbor a spoonful of hatred in your heart against someone.

It can be challenging for people to identify if they are harboring the standard form of malice in their hearts against their neighbors. How much more if it is subtle malice based on ethnicity. Does a particular Jewish man have sinful anger toward Germans in his heart? Or how about the Native American living in Oklahoma? Does he have latent malice toward white Americans? Does the South Korean boast that his people have improved themselves so that, on the whole, they are a bit better than the North Koreans? What about the black American? What about the white American? Many Christians can answer these questions with a clear conscience. They sense no animosity or superiority whatsoever. Other people, even some Christians, may have such pride or animosity within them.

If they do, there is good news. Jesus shed His blood for sinners. Jesus has made peace by the blood of His cross. Real wrongs have occurred. Genuine reconciliation has occurred because Jesus broke down the dividing wall of hostility (Ephesians 2:14). The world knows nothing of such peace. In the world's way of thinking, racism is the unforgivable sin. It is a sin that can never be admitted unless you are engaging in moral posturing and only admitting pretend racism. People do that all of the time. But, in our day, people scarcely repent of genuine racism.

This moral posturing shows the unbiblical law undergirding the new religion. The new religion rejects biblical definitions of racism. According to James Lindsey, "In Social Justice, the idea of cultural racism insists that white people maintain their social dominance and do a kind of racism to people of color by finding 'white' culture to be normal and preferable to various non-white cultures."[4] A leading anti-racist activist, Ibram Kendi, seems to track with this idea, writing, "Whoever makes the cultural standard makes the cultural hierarchy. The act of making a cultural standard and hierarchy is what creates cultural racism."[5] With these definitions, genuine racism can remain out of view. Confessing to be racist because you prefer your own culture is an excellent way to avoid confessing the real sin of racism.

The fact that racism—racial pride and racial malice—can be subtle does not mean that Christians should suspiciously scour their brothers and sisters' hearts for any traces of racism. As pastors, we have seen the destruction that comes when people give into evil surmising. One brother says another has been prideful. When he tries to explain the pride, his attempt falls flat. The pride, if there is any, is not apparent.

The Puritan, John Owen, wisely and memorably said, "Be killing sin or it will be killing you." Of course, you should first put to death your own sin before helping your fellow Christian with his. Our own logs must be removed from our eyes before we help our neighbors remove the splinters from theirs. But, even then, add another doctrine to your zeal. That doctrine is: you are not God. You do not see what He sees. You do not see the heart. Often, what you do see is obscured. In racially charged times, you should take extra care to rid yourself of any pride and malice. You should make sure you know what those sins are. Do not adopt the world's

---

4 James Lindsey, "Cultural Racism," New Discourses, July 8, 2020. https://newdiscourses.com/tftw-cultural-racism/.

5 Ibram Kendi, *How to Be an Antiracist* (New York: NY, Random House, 2019), 83.

definition of racism and then use it against your brother under the auspices of rooting out sin.

The confusion over racism is a perfect example of an opportunity for Christians to exercise responsibility. The country is obviously muddled. We do not know our right hand from our left. Some say racism is everywhere. Some say racism is nowhere. Even those who try to play the middle do not know what to do about our predicament. But we have the Word of God. We do not give in to false witnesses. Where sin is, we point it out so that people might come to know the forgiveness that is found in Jesus Christ.

To speak up on this issue requires courage. But consider the cost. We have real problems in our nation. If we pretend those problems are something that they are not, we will not solve the real issues. Even in cases where we rightly identify the problems, we need biblical solutions. Those solutions will not come from a philosophy that is antithetical to Christ. So it is our move.

Partiality

One of the courageous things that must be said is that partiality is not always wrong. Partiality can be right and good in one sense. For example, a husband ought to love his wife more than he does other women. He should be partial toward his wife in that he should have a preference for her. He should have a favorable disposition for his wife that he has for no other. Similarly, we are to do good to all people, but especially those of the household of faith (Galatians 6:10). We should privilege certain people.

In another sense, partiality is sinful (James 2:9). Sinful partiality involves undue favoring of one person or group over another. A man who treats his wife and another woman exactly the same is actually showing sinful partiality to the other woman. He bestows on her the undue favor of husbandry over against his wife, who is due that favor.

Reparations

Our nation has indeed had a troubled history when it comes to the civil relationships of black and white people. We know the slave trade was an abomination. We know sinful partiality marks our history. But the solution is not more sinful partiality. It is at precisely this point that we are confused. Some advocate for race reparations. They call for white people to pay financial reparations to descendants of slaves. The problem with race reparations is that it is stealing, a violation of the eighth commandment.

Restitution is a biblical principle. Restitution says that a man who has committed a crime against another should make some form of restoration payment to the victim. But Scripture nowhere teaches that descendants of wrongdoers should make restitution to the descendants of victims. Such a practice would be sinful partiality trying to rectify sinful partiality. But the sin of partiality can only be rectified by the blood of the cross.

Systemic Injustice

In the wake of George Floyd's death, NAACP President Derrick Johnson said, "This is not about one incident. This is about the systemic and pervasive nature of racism in this nation that must be addressed."[6] The language of "systemic" is often employed in describing our nation's racial tensions.

---

6 N'dea Yancey-Bragg, "What is systemic racism? Here's what it means and how you can help dismantle it" *USA Today*, June 19, 2020, https://www.usatoday.com/story/news/nation/2020/06/15/systemic-racism-what-does-mean/5343549002.

As the *Statement on Social Justice and the Gospel* affirmed, "All human relationships, systems, and institutions have been affected by sin."[7] So a father's sin does not only affect him. His sin impacts his family relationships, his work relationships, his church, and his civil dealings. If systemic injustice simply means that sin has affected all human systems, then there is no problem with the concept. But that meaning is not the meaning given to the term by the new religion.

Systemic racism is often defined as consisting

> of organizational culture, policies, directives, practices or procedures that exclude, displace or marginalize some racialized groups or create unfair barriers for them to access valuable benefits and opportunities. This is often the result of institutional biases in organizational culture, policies, directives, practices, and procedures that may appear neutral but have the effect of privileging some groups and disadvantaging others.[8]

There are many problems with this definition, but let us highlight one. A system is not racist merely because it results in the marginalization of a group. Marginalize can often carry the meanings to belittle or dismiss. Indeed, if your organizational culture arrogantly looks down upon certain ethnic groups, then you have a case of systemic racism. But marginalize can also mean to not be at the center, to move to the periphery. If an organization's practices and procedures

---

7 "The Statement on Social Justice and the Gospel," SJ&G, accessed October 20, 2020, https://statementonsocialjustice.com.

8 "Glossary," in "Data Standards for the Identification and Monitoring of Systemic Racism," Ontario, accessed October 20, 2020, https://www.ontario.ca/document/data-standards-identification-and-monitoring-systemic-racism/glossary.

are just, and serve a just purpose, then those practices are not racist even if certain groups are moved to the edges.

The NBA, for instance, has certain practices and procedures. As a result of those policies, white men only make up 17.9 percent of all NBA players. White people constitute about 76 percent of the nation. But they make up only 17.9 percent of our National Basketball Association. Does that mean systemic racism marks the NBA? Of course not. The directives and practices of the NBA exclude and marginalize white men. But the fact that white men are at the margins of the NBA does not mean that the NBA suffers from systemic injustice.

We have cast off responsibility for far too long. Taking responsibility in our present climate will be costly. But Christians are in the business of counting the cost, and following Jesus.

5

RULE WELL:
THE WAY TO JUSTICE IN
CIVIL RELATIONSHIPS

In America, the citizens are kings. Ours is a government of
the people, by the people, for the people. In our constitutional republic, the president is not king; neither is congress
or our supreme court. If the government goes bad, the people
are responsible for that trajectory. They must correct it. If the
people turn away from the King of Kings, setting themselves
up as the supreme kings, our form of government falls to
pieces. John Adams was right, "Our Constitution was made
only for a moral and religious People. It is wholly inadequate
to the government of any other."[1]

GUIDANCE FOR KINGS

If we would be faithful citizen kings, then we need a higher
form of guidance than the constitution. In general, the fathers
of this nation did not believe they penned the document that

---

1 John Adams, "From John Adams to Massachusetts Militia, 11 October
1798," Founders Online, October 11, 1798. https://founders.archives.gov/
documents/Adams/99-02-02-3102.

made moral and religious people. They composed the document *for* moral and religious people. If the people would be moral and religious, then they must look to the Word of the Almighty by the illumination of God's Spirit.

The Need for Guidance

America's conscience is hardened. Every human being has a conscience. The law of God, written on the human heart, informs the conscience:

> For when Gentiles, who do not have the law, by nature do what the law requires, they are a law to themselves, even though they do not have the law. They show that the work of the law is written on their hearts, while their conscience also bears witness, and their conflicting thoughts accuse or even excuse them (Romans 2:14-15).

Because of sin, the human conscience is fallible. It needs to be shaped. It needs an education. We can think something is wrong when it is not wrong. We can believe something is right when it is not right. Divine revelation instructs us. God reveals the truth in creation and Scripture.

Various societies have had more or less sensitivity to God's truth. You could find a society in which the Scripture itself is unknown. Even so, the people within that society could possess a collective conscience that is more sensitive to the divine standard than another society. For example, there was a time when the iniquity of the Amorites was not yet complete (Genesis 15:16). Then, there was a time in which their sin was complete. In their former state, the collective conscience of the Amorites was not as hardened. We are wise to take note of the varying degrees of sinfulness in different nations at different times. If you live in a society where the people make the laws, then the state of that society's conscience has an inevitable impact on their civil statutes. In present-day America, you could say that our conscience is showing. The picture is not pretty.

The church bears the responsibility to preach God's law and God's gospel. The two are not to be confused. While they are distinct, the same God who gave us the gospel also gave us the law. He loves His law as much as He loves His gospel. So, we must proclaim what God says is right and wrong, good and bad, true and false. We hold up God's standard and call people to give an account to their Creator. We do so, not saying that people must keep these laws to be acceptable to God. Instead, we say that no one can meet God's perfect standard. That is why we need the gospel. Jesus came and obeyed all of God's commandments perfectly. He suffered on the cross in place of sinners who have not kept those commandments. He did so that all who trust in Him would find acceptance with God.

God saves sinners as the church proclaims His gospel. As we observe America's hardened conscience, the church cannot point the finger and sit idly by. We must take responsibility to proclaim both God's gospel and His law. We need to disciple people in the ways of God so that, in their communities and work, they trust Jesus and obey His commands. The job can be quite daunting. You might look around and ask, "Where am I supposed to begin?" Indeed, we are dealing with decades of immoral lacquer layered on the heart of America. Nevertheless, the place where we must begin is the Word of God.

Does God have any prescriptions for kings? Of course, He does. We are not saying America is a theocracy like Old Testament Israel. But kings must rule well, justly, wisely, and seek the people's welfare under their care. That is true of all kings, not just those who ruled in the Old Testament theocratic kingdom.

GOD IS KING OF ALL THE WORLD

God is not just Lord of the church. He is Lord of the entire world. In the chapter on the civil magistrate, the 1689 Confession says, "God [is] the Supreme Lord and king of all the world."[2] The nature and implications of this truth are vast and, sadly, mostly neglected by Christians today. Since God is King of the world, all peoples and civil authorities are underneath His rule.

The confession continues by saying that our God "hath ordained civil magistrates to be under him, over the people, for His own glory in the public good."[3] Christians have not sufficiently grasped that civil authorities are under God's authority. For example, many believers lament abortion. They know it is wrong, and they call it wrong. But they have failed to see that civil authorities rebel against God when they permit abortion in their jurisdiction. It is conduct unbecoming an officer. They refuse to do the job that their Master assigned them. Many people entirely understand that a soldier in the army, who does not execute an order from the top, should be removed. If the bag boy at the local grocer refuses to bag, they expect him to be fired by the manager. But they have not seen their governors and local authorities in the same light.

The 1689 Confession teaches that presidents, judges, legislators, governors, local councils, and government officials are

---

2 *The Baptist Confession of Faith 1689* (Carlisle, PA: Banner of Truth, 2012), 24:1.
3 Ibid.

all under Jesus' rule, be they Christians or not. When the confession (in 24:1) says that civil magistrates are "under him," it refers to the triune God. Americans are accustomed to saying we are one nation under God. That language is in our pledge of allegiance. But we load that concept of "God" with whatever our imagination conjures up. However, the confession and Romans 13:4 speak clearly of Jesus Christ, our God and Savior, as being over civil authorities. It follows that these civil authorities must operate according to the instruction of the God who is over them. They are not merely to govern according to their own hardened consciences. The law of God has not stopped making people wise (Psalm 19:7).

General Equity

Along with His eternal moral law, God gave Israel both ceremonial laws and judicial laws. The ceremonial laws prefigured Christ. These ceremonial laws are no longer binding, having been taken away by Christ Himself. The judicial laws governed Israel as a body politic. These judicial laws, too, have expired with the expiration of the Old Covenant. But, there is a general equity of those judicial laws, which remains the obligation of both individuals and modern states. As the 1689 Confession puts it, the Old Testament judicial laws have "expired," with "their general equity only being of moral use."[4]

We need to recover the truth, goodness, and beauty that is found in the general equity of Israel's judicial laws. While the covenant-specific civil codes that God gave to Israel are different from the moral law written on hearts and on the tablets of stone, they are, nevertheless, full of wisdom and relevance for the United States of America. Why mention

4 Ibid., 19:4.

the relevance of these divinely established judicial laws which God gave to Israel? Why not just focus on His moral law? Because the Old Testament judicial codes can often teach us how the moral law should be applied to certain cases.

For example, we see the apostle Paul do this in 1 Corinthians 9:9-12:

> For it is written in the Law of Moses, "You shall not muzzle an ox when it treads out the grain." Is it for oxen that God is concerned? Does he not certainly speak for our sake? It was written for our sake, because the plowman should plow in hope and the thresher thresh in hope of sharing in the crop. If we have sown spiritual things among you, is it too much if we reap material things from you? If others share this rightful claim on you, do not we even more? Nevertheless, we have not made use of this right, but we endure anything rather than put an obstacle in the way of the gospel of Christ.

He builds his case for ministers of the gospel being remunerated by those who receive the benefits of their ministry on the Old Testament statute found in Deuteronomy 25:4 (see also 1 Timothy 5:17-18). The general equity of the Old Testament law was applied to taking care of the needs of gospel ministers.

The moral law, summarily comprehended in the Ten Commandments, is sadly neglected by believers and unbelievers alike. We need to meditate on that law and teach it to the nations. As we teach God's moral law, we must also think deeply on God's judicial laws to Israel found in the Old Testament. As Sam Waldron states, "Though the judicial law has expired, yet as an inspired application of the moral law to the civil circumstances of Israel it reveals many timeless principles of general equity, justice, goodness and righteousness. As such it remains relevant not only to *modern states*, but also to modern churches and Christians."[5]

Such a claim confounds many. They ask, "Are you telling me that the *judicial* laws God gave to Israel—with their stoning of sabbath breakers, instructions on leprosy, and statutes concerning the giving of a daughter in marriage—are 'relevant' to the modern Supreme Court of the United States?" The answer is yes. Had our civil leadership, at every level and in every branch, been thinking wisely in faith on such laws, as king David did, the pit in which we find ourselves would not be so deep.

We want to be clear in stating our wholehearted agreement with the 1689 Confession when it states, "To them [the Old Testament people of Israel] also he gave sundry judicial laws, which expired together with the state of that people, not obliging any now by virtue of that institution; their general equity only being of moral use."[6] We need not copy and paste the abrogated judicial laws of Israel into our modern states. Instead, we need to be rid of the secular humanism that has virtually ignored the Old Testament, disregarded the general equity of Israel's civil standards, and left us thinking that a prophetic call for our magistrates to heed God's law is somehow unwarranted by thoughtful Christians.

Several questions present themselves before the American mind at the moment. These questions concern the limits of state authority and legislation, the function of our prison system, the operation of law enforcement, slavery reparations,

---

5 Sam Waldron, *A Modern Exposition of the 1689 Baptist Confession of Faith* (Grand Rapids: EP, 2016), 284.
6 *The Baptist Confession of Faith 1689*, 19:4.

women in military combat, COVID quarantines, and the proper adjudication of crimes. To investigate answers to these pressing questions without reference to God's judicial standards to Israel would be like going to play a baseball game with one arm tied behind your back. It can be done, but why go to war without the whole counsel of God?

Do Israel's restitution laws have any relevance for our modern conversation about reparations? Does God's instruction to Israel about who needs to go to battle inform us about God's will for women in combat? Does the penal code for Israel signal anything to us about modern prisons? Can Israel's principle of *lex talionis* guide us concerning judicial sentencing? And what of Israel's quarantine statutes? Could they assist current magistrates in understanding their Master's will about an appropriate COVID response? The answer to all of these questions is a resounding *yes*.

We suspect many Christians would agree, at least in theory. Even so, they may not see our need for the wisdom in Israel's civil statutes as terribly pressing. They claim God's law is written on all men's hearts, so they already know what to do. They maintain that these "general principles of justice" are indeed *general*, which means they can be grasped by human reason without reference to Israel's specific case laws.

As noted before, the problem with such a train of thought is *America has a seared conscience*. Our collective conscience needs to be educated by God's law. We are well down the road of doing what is contrary to nature. And while the sin of the Americanites is not yet complete, we are filling up the cup at a rapid clip. It is foolish to think we can get through all of this without God's revealed wisdom.

More specifically, the law on the heart is the moral law, but that law on the heart does not detail the application of the moral law in society. Yet, the civil realm is the very place in which the magistrate rules. So, a mayor knowing, by way of conscience, that he should not steal or murder does not leave him thoroughly equipped to govern justly in the various circumstances of civil life.

Civil magistrates must make particular applications of general principles of justice. They will be the wiser for knowing Israel's judicial laws, which, though serving specific covenantal purposes, include divinely prescribed applications of the general principles of justice. While Israel's judicial laws are no longer binding on Christians or even on modern nations as nations, there is immense wisdom to be gleaned from them for both individuals and civil authorities.

Christians will have disagreements and debates about how to apply God's law in modern society. But we need to be willing to have those debates. In an effort to be pious, many Christians have relegated government and politics to a realm outside of Christian discipleship and the lordship of Christ. They may perhaps vote, but then give minimal effort to think and teach biblically on the nature and function of the state. We have let great evils persist in our land while disassociating ourselves from those evils. But the church has been called to proclaim the whole counsel of God to the whole world.

Obedience in Lawful Things

The 1689 Confession says civil magistrates are only to be obeyed in lawful things—"civil magistrates being set up by God for the ends aforesaid; subjection, in all lawful things commanded by them, ought to be yielded by us in the Lord."[7]

---

7 *The Baptist Confession of Faith 1689*, 24:3.

Upon reading this line in the confession, you must ask, "What law determines if a thing is lawful?" Some may think that civil authority should be obeyed simply because the civil authority made a law—"It must be lawful because a civil authority made it a law!" But the confession speaks to a higher law with which the civil law must accord. It is not enough to say that we are a constitutional republic, and this law is what the citizens of this republic decided to establish. If you only think of the social contract, then the confession's language of "lawful things" does not make sense.

The point is not that every civil statute has to directly and immediately tie to a Bible verse. The Scriptures will not tell you exactly where to place a four-way stop or a traffic light. But the laws of a land must be lawful according to divine revelation. That means they must have some reference to or a general consistency with what God has revealed.

Arbitrary Dictates

Some people might fall into the trap of claiming that they will not obey any law unless they can find a particular biblical command that says the same thing. Admittedly, that position is not very common in our society. But Christians should be aware of this potential mistake, which claims a civil law is unlawful when in truth, it is not.

A more common error has been the notion that civil authorities should be obeyed in all things unless there is a clear Bible verse that proves the civil order unlawful. The problem with such a position is that magistrates can establish nearly an endless list of arbitrary dictates. Such dictates may not transgress a particular Bible verse, but they are plainly arbitrary. The point is not that magistrates should leave their brains at home when they head off to work, and simply paste biblical commands into governmental mandates. The point is that they should submit their minds to what God has revealed through creation, the prophets, the apostles, and His Son.

The civil magistrate possesses a limited and regulated authority. Jesus regulates it. Far too many Christians think that the civil magistrate's authority is regulated equally by Jesus and reason, as if Jesus and human reason were co-rulers over civil authority. What we have done is put the civil authorities up there on par with Jesus to do whatever they want to do as long as they don't bump into Jesus' realm. They are permitted to legislate that all of the women dye their hair blonde because, well, there is no clear-cut biblical statute against it. They can decree that everyone 40 years old and up will wear green shirts on the 7th of August, and everyone 39 years old and down will wear blue shirts on September 12th. All kids eat broccoli on Tuesday. All men do fifteen jumping jacks each morning at 8:35 am. All executive orders are permissible so long as the civil leader stays out of Jesus' domain. The problem with such thinking is that it fails to recognize that all of creation is Jesus' domain.

Suppose the government hands down a civil law in a gray area. In that case, wisdom and patience will be required. We need to be humble in our deliberations. Pray that God would give understanding as to whether a particular law should be obeyed or respectfully resisted. Do not judge your brother or sister if they decide a different way on a challenging issue. Many have had to work through just this kind of thing with the various quarantine orders handed down by the government in different areas of our nation in the wake of the COVID virus.

Part of our considerations must include the way the magistrates themselves respond. So when you hear Nancy Pelosi had salon treatment indoors when the edict was that treatment must be outdoors, you ought to wonder if something else is going on here with this legislation. Is it really for the public good? It should shed light on our discussions when Gavin Newsom says the church cannot meet except under certain conditions, but mass protests and even riots have no such restrictions. Such things are tyranny, which Christians ought to stand against.

We are thankful to God for a constitutional republic. In a fallen world, it is a great model. But such a model does not mean that man's law is ultimate. We live in a world where human law, lower law, is nested within higher law, divine law. If the lower law transgresses the higher law, then it is not to be obeyed. If the lower law reaches the point of being plainly arbitrary, untethered from God's truth, it must be respectfully disregarded.

When you are called upon to do that, do so willing to stand for the truth. Doing so will often result in suffering. Fines or even jail may come. Disruptions to daily life are likely. We have seen this very thing happen in 2020 as civil authorities have gotten out of their lane, instructing the church about its worship.

Many problems arise when civil government becomes inflated, particularly when it grows beyond its borders to dictate church government. The 1647 Westminster Confession went too far on this point. It rightly prohibits the civil magistrate from assuming to himself the administration of the Word and sacraments. But it goes on to say that the civil magistrate

> hath authority, and it is his duty, to take order, that
> unity and peace be preserved in the Church, that the

truth of God be kept pure and entire; that all blasphemies and heresies be suppressed; all corruptions and abuses in worship and discipline prevented or reformed.[8]

It is not the place of civil government to prevent abuses in worship, much less reform them. The work of reformation and holy worship belongs to the church. The church, not the state, is "a pillar and buttress of the truth" (1 Timothy 3:15).

WHERE CITIZEN KINGS MUST START

America is in a mess. It can be quite overwhelming to find out where to begin. We ought not to think that we will fix everything in a day. But, we can start with the matter of abortion. When it comes to our nation's ills, a clear difference can be seen between the slaughter of babies and everything else.

If you are going to take God's word seriously, you cannot vote for a president who promotes the murder of children. Immigration, industry, and international policy are all critical matters. But nothing compares in significance to the abomination of abortion in our land. The civil magistrate is called by God to take the sword and punish the evildoer. He is not supposed to take the sword and execute the innocent.

Praise God for many Christians who are standing up and speaking the truth in love about abortion. They are calling upon states within the nation to no longer allow abortion within their borders. Regardless of what the Supreme Court says, the lesser magistrates throughout our land must protect life.

---

8 Westminster Divines, "The Westminster Confession of Faith (1647)," Ligonier Ministries, accessed October 28, 2020, 23:3. https://www.ligonier.org/learn/articles/westminster-confession-faith.

Democrats and Abortion

The Democratic Party platform advocates abortion. It is part of the progressive creed. There was a time when voting for the Democrat candidate was not the same as it is now. Many within the Christian community are now aware of the unholy union between the Democratic Party platform and abortion. Those who claim they can support a president who encourages the murder of children in the womb should consider if they could support Adolf Hitler. He murdered far fewer innocents in his concentration camps than Americans have in their abortion clinics.

Due to our lack of moral reasoning, we have become desensitized to what abortion is. We simply live with it. Abortion has been legal as long as many of you have been alive. It behooves the church to get clear again and speak decisively on the bloody tragedy of abortion. We are not talking about a reproductive health issue. Far too many Christians think fragmentedly about abortion. They believe it is one of many problems, but they fall into the error of moral equivalency.

The current social justice movement is proving to be a haven for hypocrisy by many who call for repentance by white evangelicals for racism. Not necessarily personal racism, mind you, but racism nonetheless as it permeates society both institutionally and systemically. That's the charge—that white evangelicals have perpetuated the sin of racism throughout society by upholding systems that have perpetuated it. One of the most prominent of those systems is national politics.

It is fascinating and infuriating that this same reasoning is not applied to what is indisputably the greatest social injustice in our society. The holocaust that is abortion has become so commonplace that some people often get upset at the mention of it when they are crusading for their own particular justice issue. This is doubly infuriating when that issue is racial injustice because over one-third of all abortions in America murder black babies. We can make a much stronger case for systemic Molechism than any we have seen for systemic racism.[9]

Think about it. Sixty million babies have been legally murdered in our nation since 1973. The current rate is nearly one million each year. Politicians like Barack Obama—the most pro-abortion United States President in history—and Hillary Clinton—who would have bumped Obama into second place had she been elected in 2016—have done more to sustain and increase this holocaust than any of their colleagues.

Despite that gruesome reality, Christian leaders have supported Obama and Clinton and encouraged their election to the highest office in the nation, all the while claiming to be advocates of "social justice." What kind of justice is it that allows a Christian blithely to promote and encourage murderous politicians? We don't have an answer to that question, but we do have this firm conviction: you can keep that perverted form of justice to yourself. We want nothing to do with it.

Our nation needs God-fearing citizen kings, who humbly look to the King of Kings. We have strayed far enough from the God under whom our nation exists.

---

9 Molech was a god of the Ammonites who required child sacrifice; see Leviticus 18:21; 2 Kings 23:10, etc. See Tom Ascol, "What's Good for Systemic Racism Is Good for Systemic Molechism," Founders Ministries, November 23, 2020. https://founders.org/2019/01/28/whats-good-for-systemic-racism-is-good-for-systemic-molechism/.

6

EMBRACE THE
FREEDOM OF SLAVERY:
THE JOY OF SLAVERY TO CHRIST

If we are to follow Christ amid the rise of America's new religion, then we must get comfortable doing things that are anathema to that new religion. They called our Lord a blasphemer. As He told us, "It is enough for the disciple to be like his teacher, and the servant like his master. If they have called the master of the house Beelzebul, how much more will they malign those of his household" (Matthew 10:25). One of those accursed practices, which the new religion cannot abide, and we must perform, is the joyful embracing of slavery.

Remember that the new religion says you are autonomous, beholden to no one. The tyrants rule over you, of course. But they do so by pretending to give you liberty. The spirit of anarchy drives the new religion. Such a spirit will not take on chains. The apostle Paul, however, says, "Thanks be to God, that you who were once slaves of sin have become obedient from the heart to the standard of teaching to which you were committed, and, having been set free from sin, have become slaves of righteousness" (Romans 6:17-18).

But we must not embrace every kind of slavery. We have a particular type of chain to receive joyfully. It is the chain of Christ, the slavery of righteousness. The new religion has its own form of slavery. Civil leaders have begun to mandate the details of your family Thanksgiving.[1] At heart, the new religion is enslaved to sin. We must have nothing to do with *that* slavery. But we do have a glorious slavery to embrace. It is the freest slavery imaginable, slavery to Christ and His ways.

THE IDOLATRY OF CHOICE

The creed goes, "My body, my choice." Some recite the creed in an attempt to support abortion. In such a case, the rationale does not hold up since the baby, while located in the mother's body, is not the mother's body. The motto, however, has run off in other directions, attempting to support another troubling movement. Some claim it supports the LGBTQ agenda. It is, after all, your body. Do you not get to choose your own sex? This question was inconceivable only a couple of generations ago. But it is not any longer. Our culture has succumbed to the idolatry of choice.

Christians must not look down their noses at a society that has begun to reap the bitter fruit of worshiping personal choice. We have been down that road. We regularly repent of that very idolatry—"All we like sheep have gone astray; we have turned—every one—to his own way; and the LORD has laid on him the iniquity of us all" (Isaiah 53:6). But Christians, having received the grace of God, do have the ability to repent of choosing our own way. We know how to

---

1 David Eggert and Rachel La Corte, "Governors ratchet up restrictions ahead of Thanksgiving," AP News, November 16, 2020, https://apnews. com/article/travel-family-gatherings-coronavirus-pandemic-thanksgiving-holidays-3c759ab924a0d9de27803527ddf36c1c.

live as created beings with limitations, acknowledging that we are not God.

We see the idolatry of choice in all fallen human creatures. We see it when children say, "You are not the boss of me." They do not like restraint or limitations. God gives children parents, in part, so that they can learn the boundaries of their humanity. They can learn they are not God. They need to learn these things to live the way God has created them to live. We see this tendency more broadly in the ever-present goal of being true to yourself. To be true to yourself, you must pursue your will regardless of what God says about the matter. Such a pursuit is a sinful one. Christians have been liberated from that sinful pursuit. Once, we were slaves to sin. But now we say with Christ, "Not my will, but yours, be done" (Luke 22:42).

The new religion, marked by the idolatry of choice, cannot abide submission to God's Word. For example, God has made them male and female. But we insist that human beings can choose their own sexuality, and even identity, without consequences. This spirit was evident in a recent Supreme Court decision in which Justice Neil Gorsuch wrote the opinion.

GORSUCH: BOSTOCK SUPREME COURT DECISION

In Bostock v. Clayton County, Georgia (2020), the Supreme Court ruled that federal law forbids employers from firing employees because of their sexual identity or orientation. Justice Gorsuch found that such an action transgressed Title VII of the Civil Rights Act of 1964. The text of that particular act of Congress states,

> It shall be an unlawful employment practice for an
> employer—to fail or refuse to hire or to discharge any
> individual, or otherwise to discriminate against any
> individual with respect to his compensation, terms,
> conditions, or privileges of employment, because of
> such individual's race, color, religion, sex, or national
> origin.[2]

Gorsuch reasoned that an employer discharging a biological man because he thinks and acts as if he were a woman
is to terminate him because of his sex, thus a transgression
of Title VII. Likewise, Gorsuch found it a violation of Title
VII for an employer to discharge a biological man because he
wants to or does have sex with another man.

Gorsuch was wrong. An employer who fires a man because
he pretends to be a woman is not firing him because he is a
man, but because he is pretending to be a woman. Likewise,
an employer who fires a man because he has sex with another
man is not firing him because he is a man, but because he is
having sex with another man. Justice Gorsuch was wrong to
opine that such cases transgressed Title VII.

But his faulty justification demonstrates just how far the
idolatry of choice has progressed in our society. Gorsuch,
referring to the Title VII statute, argues,

> The statute's message for our cases is equally simple
> and momentous: An individual's homosexuality or
> transgender status is not relevant to employment

---

2 "2011 US Code Title 42 - The Public Health and Welfare Chapter 21
- CIVIL RIGHTS (§§ 1981 - 2000h-6) Subchapter VI - EQUAL EM-
PLOYMENT OPPORTUNITIES (§§ 2000e - 2000e-17) Section 2000e-
2 - Unlawful employment practices," JUSTIA US Law, November 21, 2020,
https://law.justia.com/codes/us/2011/title-42/chapter-21/subchapter-vi/
section-2000e-2.

decisions. That's because it is impossible to discriminate against a person for being homosexual or transgender without discriminating against that individual based on sex. Consider, for example, an employer with two employees, both of whom are attracted to men. The two individuals are, to the employer's mind, materially identical in all respects, except that one is a man and the other a woman. If the employer fires the male employee for no reason other than the fact he is attracted to men, the employer discriminates against him for traits or actions it tolerates in his female colleague.[3]

In other words, Gorsuch claims that the employer must have transgressed the "sex" standard of Title VII because you cannot discriminate against a person practicing homosexuality "without discriminating against that individual *based on sex*" (emphasis ours). This claim is an evasion of plain truth in order to avoid the wrath that comes from offending the idol of choosing one's sexual identity and lifestyle.

Certainly, Gorsuch is correct that you cannot even know that an individual is homosexual or transgender without reference to sex (biology at birth). But, taking note of one's sex is an entirely different thing than "discriminating against any individual... because of such individual's sex," as the law states. Justice Alito made this very point in his dissent, saying,

> In an effort to prove its point, the Court carefully includes in its example just two employees, a homosexual man and a heterosexual woman, but suppose we add two more individuals, a woman who is

---

3 Bostock v. Clayton County, 590 U.S. ___ (2020).

attracted to women and a man who is attracted to women. (A large employer will likely have applicants and employees who fall into all four categories, and a small employer can potentially have all four as well.) We now have the four exemplars listed below, with the discharged employees crossed out:

~~Man attracted to men~~

Woman attracted to men

~~Woman attracted to women~~

Man attracted to women

The discharged employees have one thing in common. It is not biological sex, attraction to men, or attraction to women. It is attraction to members of their own sex—in a word, sexual orientation. And that, we can infer, is the employer's real motive.[4]

The reasoning Justice Gorsuch has supplied is problematic on many fronts. For example, he would bar an employer from granting any maternity leave. The employer would not be able to do that without reference to the biology of the employee. All employee restroom and shower policies regarding sex are gone. As it pertains to "terms, conditions, or privileges of employment," any reference to male or female is unlawful. What are the implications for prison employees and inmates? Perhaps when LeBron James retires from the NBA, he can go play for the WNBA and have several more years as a professional player. This reasoning is an attack upon God's image-bearers, and therefore it is an attack upon God himself and the way that He created the world.

---

4 Ibid. (Alito, dissenting).

Gorsuch's argument implies that we must now look at each other, not as man or woman, male or female. We must look at each other as skin and bones with gray matter. As an employer, you must decide if you will hire a particular set of skin, bones, and gray matter to do a job. When a Justice of the Supreme Court has forbidden not only prejudice based on sex, but any reference to sex, then you know the idolatry of choice is deeply rooted in that society. This notion rejects God's good created order. God created us male and female. To suggest that being a man or woman has no bearing upon one's essential personhood is basically to say there is no God. It is a claim that we are God. We will determine what is essential to humanity and what is not. The idolatry of choice has trumped biological truth. The idea is Orwellian. If the truth about my biology is not relevant to our interactions with one another, what other truths are irrelevant?

Here we see how beautiful slavery to Christ is. It is slavery to the truth and freedom from lies. The Christian faith enables one to live in the real world. We do not have to manipulate. We do not need to attempt a great twisting of God's wisely established world. It is in slavery to Christ that we find freedom and joy. It is crucial that we rightly understand slavery and freedom.

SLAVERY TO SIN

Jesus identifies mankind's slavery in John 8:34 when He says, "Truly, truly, I say to you, everyone who practices sin is a slave to sin." We know from the rest of the Bible that everyone is in view here. It is not as if only some people practice sin and thus are slaves to sin. Romans 3:23 says, "All have sinned." Some have been liberated; others remain in sin's chains. But it does us all good to consider our slavery whether it is a past reality or a present one. What does Jesus mean when He says we are enslaved to sin?

He reveals that we are enslaved to the power of sin. Christ tells the Jews that the one who practices sin cannot stop. Sin has power over him. Sin has mastered him and continues to master him. Many people struggle to think of themselves as mastered by sin. We consider ourselves survivors and achievers. But we are not. Ephesians 2:1 says we are dead in sin, following the prince of the power of the air. Sin has a deadening power on us. We can work, fight, pray, read, but, left to ourselves, we lack the strength to escape the shackles of sin.

We are not only enslaved to sin, but entirely enslaved to it. Sin's slavery is all-encompassing. It permeates every aspect of our lives. The earthly slave is a slave no matter what he is doing. He is a slave when he wakes in the morning. He is a slave when he eats. He is a slave when he works. He is a slave when he walks along the road. He is a slave when he reads. He is a slave when he lies down to sleep at night. In the same way, the slave to sin is always a slave.

One reason for so many self-help books at the bookstore is we have underestimated how dire our situation is. We like to think of our sins as if they were no more than minor shortcomings. Or we speak of areas of improvement as if some other areas are improved enough. We consider our sin like a bruise on an otherwise perfectly good apple. But, the truth is, apart from Christ, we are rotten to the core. Romans 3 says we have not only sinned but become worthless.

As slaves to sin, we are enslaved to do sin's bidding. Scripture tells us that the Jews were trying to kill Jesus. This murderous desire is a sign of their slavery to sin. Sin kills, and they wanted to kill. The wages of sin is death. The earthly slave must do what the master desires, and so it is with slavery to sin. Paul says this is what goes on with those who oppose the gospel. He says the devil has captured them to do his will (2 Timothy 2:26). The slave to sin is an agent of the wicked one. He is not neutral. You can understand why the Jews responded with offense when Jesus told them they were slaves to sin (John. 8:33). But their offense shows us another dimension of sin's slavery.

Humanity is deceptively enslaved to sin. The Jews were thoroughly convinced they were not slaves. They object to Jesus, "We are offspring of Abraham and have never been enslaved to anyone" (John 8:33)! But they, in fact, were enslaved. Sin wound its chains around them in the dark. Jesus had told them previously that they were walking in darkness. Romans 1 says that by our unrighteousness, we suppress the truth. Sin's mastery over fallen humanity is a truth that we are quite good at suppressing. We might exchange one vice for another to reassure ourselves and others that we are in control. We change out disreputable sins for respectable sins, fooling ourselves into thinking we are not in chains. The devil is perfectly happy to have us play this game. He smiles when we think our biggest slavery problem is people stopping us from doing what we want. In such a mindset, we are distracted from our real slavery to sin.

While we are deceptively enslaved to sin, it is also true that we are willingly enslaved. Jesus once said to the Jews, "I speak of what I have seen with my Father, and you do what you have heard from your father" (John 8:38). He went on to tell them plainly that they were sons of the devil. The enslaved sinner desires sin. He is not kept against his will. Mankind's slavery is a heart slavery. We are lured and enticed to sin by our own desire (James 1:14). So the old excuse that the devil made me do it falls flat.

Our slavery to sin includes slavery to sin's punishment. Anyone who stays in Satan's chains will suffer Satan's fate. Satan, and those who follow him, will one day be thrown into the lake of fire, "and they will be tormented day and night forever and ever" (Revelation 20:10). Psalm 7:12 says, "If a man does not repent, God will whet His sword; He has bent and readied His bow."

There is, however, a Liberator who can set people free.

JESUS THE LIBERATOR

There is hope in the Liberator. His name is Jesus. He sets sinners free from their miserable slavery to sin. John 8:36 says, "If the *Son* sets you free, you will be free indeed." What does it mean that Jesus is the sin-liberating Son of God?

As the Son of God, Jesus has the power to liberate. To appreciate Christ's power, we need to tune in to what the Bible says about heavenly or spiritual power. There are evil heavenly authorities who are quite powerful. We hear about them in Colossians 2:15. We also hear there that Jesus disarms them. But, if Jesus disarms them, that means that apart from Jesus, they are armed. These authorities are cosmic powers over this present darkness. They are spiritual forces of evil in the heavenly places (Ephesians 6:12). In other words, there are real evil beings keeping sinners in bondage, beings that are far more powerful than any of us. But, they are not stronger than Christ. He has put them to open shame by triumphing over them. Hebrews 2:14 says that the devil has the power of death, but Jesus has destroyed him. Jesus has the power to liberate us from evil spiritual rulers, from sin itself, from the devil, and death.

Along with His power, Jesus has the authority to liberate. You may often find a person who has the power to do something but not the authority to do it. You can find a contractor who has all the ability to renovate your house, but he is not licensed in the state. Or, you might find a man perfectly able to govern a city, but he lacks the necessary credentials and therefore does not have the right to do so. Jesus, being the Son of God, has not only the power but also the right to emancipate us from sin's slavery. Jesus says God gave Him this authority. God gave Him authority over all flesh, to give eternal life to all the Father has given Him (John 17:2). Some Christians can be so assaulted by the enemy that they begin to believe his lies, "It is not right for you to be free." But it is perfectly right for the Christian to be free because he has been justly liberated. Jesus has every credential necessary to walk into the kingdom of darkness and walk out with the children of God.

As the Son of God, Jesus has the truth to liberate. If you would be liberated from sin's deceit, you must encounter the truth. Lies cannot deliver you from lies. Falsehood cannot deliver you from falsehood. If any person is going to be set free from sin, then he must see the truth about his sin. He must see the truth about God. He must see the truth about himself. But a man can only come to know these things through the Word of Christ, who is the truth. Jesus says, "If you abide in my word, you are truly my disciples, and you will know the truth, and the truth will set you free" (John 8:31). Our only hope is that the truth of Christ finds a place in us. If the Word of Christ glances off of you, then you are still in slavery. If the Word of Christ abides in you, then you are free indeed.

Jesus purchased our liberty. He was not only the right man for the job. He did the job. We know that freedom is not free. If you are going to unchain slaves, then you have to buy them. The cost of our liberty was Christ's blood. Jesus said that He was the one who had authority to lay down His life; no one took it from Him. No one did anything to Him that He did not command to be done.

Make no mistake: Jesus is the only liberator. The Jews claimed another liberator. They thought being Abraham's physical sons could save them. We are tempted to do the same today. We seek liberation through guilt-bearing, through good-doing, through successful careera, through happy families, through healthy eating, through social media affirmation, through educational advancement. But the apostle's message is still true, "And there is salvation in no one else, for there is no other name under heaven given among men by which we must be saved" (Acts 4:12). When we know this Christ savingly, we become His slaves. And becoming His slaves makes us free indeed.

FREE INDEED

Our everyday talk about liberty often leaves out what we are free to do. But God does not leave us in the dark about the sweetness of our freedom. When Jesus says we will be free indeed, He means we will be really free. What does it mean to be really and truly free?

Christians are free from the guilt of having broken God's law. We are free to live in Christ's righteousness which He earned by keeping God's law. Through faith, we have been given this righteousness to wear as a breastplate. We do not have to walk around in the endless guilt of the new religion. We are righteous in Christ. In God's sight we are as we ought to be. This truth brings fresh air and new confidence. We will not be able to navigate the days ahead without it.

Our freedom includes being free from sin's dominion. In Christ we are now free to exercise dominion over sin by putting it to death in our own lives and exposing and renouncing it everywhere. Christians are free to stand against the evil that they once embraced and had rule over them. The tables have been turned. Romans 6:14 says, "sin shall have no more dominion over you." Then we are told, "put to death what is earthly in you" (Colossians 3:5). Kill it. You have the liberty to kill what you could not kill before. The Spirit lives in you. The Word of God abides in you. You are free to identify sin—sight in your spiritual weapons. And blow sin away. You are free to fight sin and win.

Furthermore, we are free from shame so that we can experience glory. Shame is not the same thing as guilt. Shame is the disgrace that sin brings. But, Jesus bore that shame for His children. He suffered our shame. He was despised and disgraced for our sin. Our sin is now gone, and the shame with it. Isaiah 61:7 speaks of the year of the Lord's favor, which is upon us in Christ. It says, "Instead of your shame there shall be a double portion; instead of dishonor they shall rejoice in their lot." Christians are free to live in the joy and glory of God. We are free not to hide our faces but to walk with our heads held high in Christ. We are free to behold the glory of the Lord and be transformed into the same image from one degree of glory to another (2 Corinthians 3:18).

Our freedom includes freedom from condemnation unto communion with God. Romans 8:1 says, "There is therefore now no condemnation for those who are in Christ Jesus." Instead of furious judgment, we are free to know the favor of God. We are free to walk with Him. We are free to sit down with Him at table. We are free to feast with Christ, sit at His feet, learn from Him, and draw near Him. God is our God. We are His sons and daughters.

Happy Slaves

David says in Psalm 16:5-6, "The LORD is my chosen portion and my cup; you hold my lot. The lines have fallen for me in pleasant places; indeed, I have a beautiful inheritance." When we have that mindset, we will be delighted to do whatever God has given us to do. By faith, David knew the slavery that liberates. He knew the Messiah, who has now come accomplishing our salvation. Trusting Christ, we can live as joyful slaves of righteousness, going about our work with a song amid a grumpy world. If you are working in a particular industry, then praise God and work diligently by faith. If you are a homemaker, then you will joyfully go about the labor. If you are a grandmother or grandchild, a son or a daughter, a boss or an employee, a man or a woman, find joy in the slavery to Christ that liberates.

At the root of all of this either faith or unbelief. We either trust the God who is, or we do not. If we trust him, we will find in Him our great reward. We will learn increasingly to be content in whatever condition we find ourselves. Why? Because if I am poor, I have Christ. If I am wealthy, I have Christ. If I am healthy, I have Christ. If I am sick, I have Christ. And if I have Christ, I have everything.

7

FACE THE DANGER: THE COURAGE TO GO TO A REBEL WORLD

In C. S. Lewis' *The Lion, the Witch, and the Wardrobe*, young Lucy and Susan discover that Aslan was not exactly who they thought he was. Mr. Beaver tells them,

> "Aslan is a lion—*the* Lion, the great Lion." "Ooh" said Susan. "I'd thought he was a man. Is he—quite safe? I shall feel rather nervous about meeting a lion." "That you will dearie, and no mistake," said Mrs. Beaver; "If there's anyone who can appear before Aslan without their knees knocking, they're either braver than most or else just silly." "Then he isn't safe?" said Lucy. "Safe?" said Mr. Beaver; "don't you hear what Mrs. Beaver tells you? Who said anything about safe? 'Course he isn't safe. But he's good. He's the King, I tell you."[1]

We do not follow a safe King. It was not safe coming to a fallen world. Neither was it safe to go to the cross. He has told us plainly what we are to do, "If anyone would come after me,

---

1 C. S. Lewis, *The Lion, the Witch, and the Wardrobe* (New York: Harper Collins, 1950), 79-80.

let him deny himself and take up his cross and follow me. For whoever would save his life will lose it, but whoever loses his life for my sake will find it" (Matthew 16:24-25).

At this point, the lay of the land is before us. We must follow Jesus amid the rise of America's new religion. That religion involves a hardened secularism, manifesting itself in Critical Theory and Social Justice in all of their various forms and offshoots. This religion proclaims a false hope of autonomy and universal equality. It is governed by tyrants and fueled by anarchy. As we advance with Christ, we must rule well, looking to His law as citizen kings. We also must take responsibility to speak the truth in love amid lawlessness and confusion. Faithfulness requires embracing a form of slavery that liberates, namely slavery to Christ and His righteousness.

It is not hard to see that the road ahead requires courage. The defensive measures and offensive measures require us to face the danger. And facing danger is not something with which American Christianity is terribly familiar. We have found many ways to ignore the danger or hide from the danger. We have raised a generation on youth group skits and entertainment, failing to prepare them for the cost and battle of public witness to Christ. N. D. Wilson has articulated a clear vision for raising the next generation to face the chaotic world:

> The world is rated R, and no one is checking IDs. Do not try to make it G by imagining the shadows away. Do not try to hide your children from the world forever, but do not try to pretend there is no danger. Train them. Give them sharp eyes and bellies full of laughter. Make them dangerous. Make them

yeast, and when they've grown, they will pollute the shadows.[2]

Our failure to raise up a generation according to this vision stems from our unwillingness to face the danger.

Everett Piper highlighted just this problem and how it has been unveiled through the COVID pandemic. He explained,

> The greatest challenge the American experiment faces in this dark hour is not our need for safety but our loss of liberty. And the complicity of the church in the wholesale abandonment of this self-evident truth is no less than stunning. While governors across the nation fall over themselves to break their oath of office, the church remains quiet. While one mayor after another assumes unilateral power, pastors across the spectrum of denominations shame rather than applaud those who resist such demagogic arrogance.[3]

Piper goes on to identify the bitter fruit that grows when safety becomes our chief aim:

> If anything is clear in the history of civilization, as well as that of the church, it is this: When you sacrifice human freedom for the sake of human safety, you almost always diminish the human being. Citizens of the former Soviet Union, for example, may have been "safe," but this was not the stuff of personal dignity and worth. As the old axiom goes, "A ship in the

---

2 N. D. Wilson, *Notes from the Tilt-A-Whirl: Wide-Eyed Wonder in God's Spoken World* (Nashville: Thomas Nelson, 2009), 157.

3 Everett Piper, "Greatest threat America faces during COVID-19 pandemic is loss of liberty," *The Washington Times*, April 18, 2020, https://www.washingtontimes.com/news/2020/apr/18/greatest-threat-america-faces-during-COVID-19-pand.

harbor is safe, but that's not what ships are for," and so it is with human beings. Safety at the expense of freedom always degrades rather than elevates what it means to be made in the image of God. Michael Ramsden (from the Oxford Center for Christian Apologetics) recently argued that the greatest threat to human beings in the 21st century could, in fact, be a misguided concept of human safety.[4]

A Heritage of Facing the Danger

The Christian life is not safe, but it is good. God promises goodness to us. He has given us everything that we need for this life and the life to come. Every blessing in heavenly places already belongs to us in Christ. The Christian community has understood these precious truths. Throughout history, these promises fueled their courage to face the danger. They lived by faith, and that is risky in a fallen world.

Why would Abraham give up his homeland and go to a country he did not know? The familiarity of home provides security. But God said for him to go, so he went. The apostle Paul rhetorically asked, "Why are we in danger every hour" (1 Corinthians 15:30)? He fought with beasts at Ephesus, speaking about people, not animals. He exclaimed, "I die every day" (1 Corinthians 15:31)! Why would Moses go and face Pharaoh, the most powerful king in the region who could take his life? Why would Joshua go into the Promised Land to conquer the giants in the land? Why in the world would Esther go before King Ahasuerus, risking her life and her people? Why would Mordecai not just bend the knee before Haman? The answer to all of these questions is: Jesus is risen from the dead, and we, too, will rise from the dead.

---

4 Ibid.

We must not advance in these days without a clear grasp of this fundamental truth: There is a world to come. We have a life beyond death, beyond the grave. Speaking to the Ephesians elders, Paul said in Acts 20:24, "I do not account my life of any value nor as precious to myself, if only I may finish my course and the ministry that I received from the Lord Jesus, to testify to the gospel of the grace of God." In the next chapter, people beg him not to go to Jerusalem as Agabus tells him of the trouble he will encounter. Paul responds, "What are you doing, weeping and breaking my heart? For I am ready not only to be imprisoned but even to die in Jerusalem for the name of the Lord Jesus" (Acts 21:13). If we have that mentality, then the fearmongering and shaming that are becoming increasingly present in our society will have no power over us.

On Earth as It Is in Heaven

The old adage, "You can become so heavenly minded you are no earthly good," needs a slight adjustment. It should read, "You can become so confused about heaven you are no earthly good." The problem with the saying is that it is not too much heavenly-mindedness that leaves you doing no earthly good. Instead, it is misguided notions about heaven that leave people doing no earthly good. The nub of our problem is thinking that the two, heaven and earth, are entirely unrelated. The error is easy to make because the two are indeed distinct. Heaven is not earth, and earth is not heaven. They are, nonetheless, very much related.

Many Christians in America have found a way to hope in heaven that leaves them not facing up to the danger on earth. In other words, they claim they are seeking a better and heavenly country, but that eye toward the heavenly country leaves them not trusting and obeying God down here. It was just the opposite for Abraham and our other examples in the hall of faith. Indeed, they acknowledged they were "strangers and exiles on earth" (Hebrews 11:13). They desired a heavenly country (Hebrews 11:16). But their faith always produced faithful living on earth. Because of their heavenly gaze, they could see things accurately on earth and follow Jesus.

So Noah built the ark with wood, splinters and all. Sarah conceived and suffered labor pains. Abraham put his feet on the pathway, leaving his home. Rahab hid the spies. Consider all of the earthy things done by faith in the heavenly country:

> And what more shall I say? For time would fail me to tell of Gideon, Barak, Samson, Jephthah, of David and Samuel and the prophets—who through faith conquered kingdoms, enforced justice, obtained promises, stopped the mouths of lions, quenched the power of fire, escaped the edge of the sword, were made strong out of weakness, became mighty in war, put foreign armies to flight. Women received back their dead by resurrection. Some were tortured, refusing to accept release, so that they might rise again to a better life. Others suffered mocking and flogging, and even chains and imprisonment. They were stoned, they were sawn in two, they were killed with the sword. They went about in skins of sheep and goats, destitute, afflicted, mistreated—of whom the world was not worthy—wandering about in deserts and mountains, and in dens and caves of the earth (Hebrews 11:32-38).

As all of these faith-filled Christians faced the danger, they served the coming of Christ's kingdom on earth. Jesus taught us to pray, "Your kingdom come, your will be done, on earth as it is in heaven" (Matthew 6:10). They understood the relationship between heaven and earth. The relationship is one in which earth is increasingly experiencing the coming of God's kingdom and will. Therefore, faith in God cannot lead to the neglect of God's will and kingdom on earth. The objection comes, "But, it will be perilous to follow God's ways without qualification amid the rise of America's new religion. We may lose job, reputation, freedoms, opportunities, or worse." And the answer to the objection follows, "Precisely. But you seek a heavenly country. So face the danger."

Scripture ought to orient our lives. And the Scripture signals that we are to face the danger and go to the world. In the beginning, God created Adam and Eve. He gave them direction. They were to be fruitful and multiply, fill the earth, and have dominion (Genesis 1:28). They were to work and keep the Garden while expanding their work, spreading God's image as they advanced. Whatever the exact nature of that pre-fallen world, our first parents still had to fill, subdue, and have dominion. The job was not to sit around and wait. After the flood, Noah received the same kind of instruction from God—"And God blessed Noah and his sons and said to them, 'Be fruitful and multiply and fill the earth'" (Genesis 9:1). In the wake of that dreadful judgment, Noah was to produce, work, pray, trust God, and spread again the image of God over the wide earth.

We are sons of Adam and daughters of Eve. Noah is father of us all. God's instruction to multiply, fill, subdue and rule has not fallen to the ground. In Christ, we have a fuller understanding of what God would have us do. Jesus echoed this first instruction in a greater way when He said upon His resurrection,

All authority in heaven and on earth has been given
to me. Go therefore and make disciples of all nations,
baptizing them in the name of the Father and of the
Son and of the Holy Spirit, teaching them to observe
all that I have commanded you. And behold, I am
with you always, to the end of the age (Matthew
28:18-20).

Thank God that Jesus is with us. Because that Great
Commission is a hazardous one. Consider what happened to
those apostles who received it firsthand. They suffered and
died to fulfill Christ's call.

The book of Acts is filled with examples of the church facing peril. They did not remain in Jerusalem but spread, going
to a rebel world. It was costly to live for Christ in Jerusalem.
And it was costly to live for Christ in Thessalonica. Ephesus
was no safe haven. Rome provided no harbor. Corinth was
not a paradise for Christianity. There is good reason why
theologians speak of the church militant. You need to look
no further than the book of Acts to see why.

For far too long, many American Christians have maintained a false concept of evangelism. Our evangelistic strate-
gy looks nothing like the apostles' approach. It looks nothing
like the Early Church, the church of the Middle Ages, or the
Reformation. We believe we will advance the kingdom by
being liked. Niceness has subbed in for a faithful witness to
the Savior. The underlying problem is that we trust in our
ability to package Jesus rather than His ability to save sinners.

We need to recover a vision of the position and progress of
Christ displayed in Psalm 110. There we hear that Jesus will
sit at the right hand of the Father until His enemies are made
His footstool. As He sits, God advances His truth throughout the world.

The Position and Progress of King Jesus

When it comes to the church's great mission in the world, we can feel as if we are on the losing team more often than not. We hear the latest news headlines and despairingly ask, "What is the world coming to?" After a disheartened sigh, we reminisce a little about the days when people worked harder, consumed less, held marriage in honor, and children obeyed their parents.

Leaving off for the moment the superficiality of nostalgic tendencies to romanticize past eras, the question we need to ask ourselves is this: "Are we really on the losing team?" Or to put a finer point on it, "Is Jesus a coach gathering us up with the encouragement that we are probably not going to win, but we should show the other team that we have heart?" Scripture portrays another picture. David speaks of the present position of Christ in Psalm 110:1, saying, "The LORD says to my Lord: 'Sit at my right hand until I make your enemies your footstool.'"

Christ's position is one of honor. To sit at the right hand is to sit in a prominent place. It is this high position to which the Father exalted the Son. Jesus has always been worthy of honor, but David here speaks of the Son's exaltation upon His ascension. Paul speaks of the same in Philippians 2, saying that after Christ's death, the Father has now highly exalted the Son and bestowed on Him the name that is above every name.

The Lord Himself has said for King Jesus to take this position. In a beautiful example of humility, Christ did not take this position of His own accord. He was fully worthy of it. Even so, it is the Father who exalted Him to the position that

He rightly deserved. The King enthroned at the right hand of God is a humble King.

The King's position signifies his finished work. Jesus is not standing but sitting at the right hand of the Father. Sitting is what we do when we have finished a job. As Christ laid down His perfect life on the cross, He spoke these words, "It is finished" (John 19:30). All that God had given Him to do had been done. The salvation of His people was accomplished. All of the obedience required had been fulfilled. All of the wrath which needed to be suffered had been suffered. The serpent's head was crushed. The evil rulers were put to open shame, and Christ sat down in victory.

The King's position is one of authority. The fact that Jesus is sitting indicates His right to rule. He is seated at a lofty position. When kings do this kind of thing, it means they are seated on a throne. How different is the picture in Matthew 28 after the death and resurrection of Christ than the one of Jesus is in the wilderness being tempted by Satan? Satan offers Jesus all the kingdoms of this world and their glory in exchange for Jesus' worship in the wilderness. In Matthew 28, Jesus has all authority in heaven and on earth.

The King's position does not bode well for His enemies. Even though Christ is highly exalted after accomplishing redemption, He does still have enemies. There are those who quite foolishly oppose this meek and exalted King. What comes of them? What is coming of them right now? They are becoming Christ's footstool. We do not have to wait around for a day when this will happen. This subjection is happening now. The King will sit at the right hand of the Father until the full subduing is accomplished.

David not only marks the position of Jesus but His progress as well. He says, "The LORD sends forth from Zion your mighty scepter. Rule in the midst of your enemies" (Psalm 110:2)! Jesus has not only ascended to sit at the right hand of the Father. He also conquers on earth through His Spirit's power.

He goes forth from Zion. The prophets of the Old Testament use Zion as a common reference for Jerusalem. Amos 1:2 says, "The Lord roars from Zion and utters His voice from Jerusalem." Micah 4:2 echoes Psalm 110, "For out of Zion shall go forth the law, and the word of the Lord from Jerusalem." Jesus continues the idea in Acts 1:8 when He says, "You will receive power when the Holy Spirit comes upon you, and you will be my witnesses in Jerusalem and in all Judea and Samaria, and to the ends of the earth." It was in Jerusalem that Christ laid down His life and rose again. It was in Jerusalem that the Holy Spirit came upon the church in power. It was in Jerusalem that the church of Christ was first established. And it was from Jerusalem that the Spirit-empowered church took the mighty gospel of God to the nations.

This gospel is still spreading. Two thousand years ago, something so significant happened in Jerusalem that the world will never again be the same. What occurred there is good news. Jesus Christ, the Son of God, was born of a virgin. He fully obeyed all of God's law, died for sinners, and rose again, never to die again. This Jesus is still alive today and can save to the uttermost those who come to Him in faith. This message is the power of God for salvation.

We should anticipate Christ's rule and live in the light of it. Jesus goes forth as a King. Kings rule. When Jesus conquers a person, that person changes. Undoubtedly, the complete change does not occur in a moment. The rule of Christ does not come overnight or in an instant like when you switch on a light. But He does conquer the human heart by His grace, and thoroughly so. Jesus commissioned His followers to go into the world and teach others to observe what He commands. People from all nations are not only to learn His ways but submit to them. David tells us that we can anticipate this kind of thing in the world.

While we anticipate Christ's rule, we must also acknowledge that the King progresses in the midst of His enemies. We should not assume that such an advance will be easy. Advance always comes at a cost. We ought not to lose heart when we meet those who oppose King Jesus and His ways. In those encounters, we experience exactly what God has promised would happen.

Our King plays offense. God is not back on his heels. He is not trying to run out the clock until half-time so He can regroup. He is on the attack. And He calls us to join Him.

WHETHER BY LIFE OR BY DEATH

The only way to face the danger is to see that God controls the danger. Things are dangerous out there because He rules the world that way. Amid the COVID virus, many people focused on secondary causes. They analyzed data. They listened to epidemiologists. While there is nothing wrong with data (accurate data, that is)—it is, after all, God's world—there is a problem with focusing on secondary causes to the neglect of primary causes. We ought to remember that pestilence has been known to stop working because God told the angel working the pestilence to stay his hand (2 Samuel 24:16). That revealed truth is just as real as the accurate data cultivated through observation of the physical world.

If the church is not going to speak for God, who is? If Christians do not announce what God has done, then it will not be announced. Until we firmly grasp the truth that our loving God controls every molecule that exists, we will be easily manipulated by calls for safety. We certainly encourage people to be wise. People find themselves in different situations. We should look on people's varying decisions with humility and charity. We do not know all of the details about a person's life. The call is not to be reckless, but it is to face the danger, whether it be the remarkably small likelihood of dying from COVID or any other spiritual or physical danger that comes upon us in life.

We should make it our goal to die well. It is good to remember that you are going to die. Christians need not fear death. We say with the apostle, "'Death is swallowed up in victory.' 'O death, where is your victory? O death, where is your sting?' The sting of death is sin, and the power of sin is the law. But thanks be to God, who gives us the victory through our Lord Jesus Christ" (1 Corinthians 15:54-56). It is no surprise that Paul immediately follows this triumph over death with a call to "be steadfast, immovable, always abounding in the work of the Lord" (1 Corinthians 15:58). The one who does not fear death can steadfastly abound in the work of the Lord.

Making people fear death is one of the devil's greatest strategies. In one sense it is completely understandable that mortal creatures fear the end of their mortal lives. Death is the experience that neither you nor we have personally experienced. Paul calls it the "last enemy" (1 Corinthians 15:26). For the Christian, it is an enemy that has been defeated and that will one day—at the return of Christ—will be completely destroyed. Through His death, Jesus conquered death and that conquest, as we embrace it, think rightly about it, and remember it, does in fact set believers free from being terrorized by death.

The author of Hebrews specifically makes this point as he extols the greatness of Jesus in the second chapter of his letter. He writes,

> Since therefore the children share in flesh and blood, he himself likewise partook of the same things, that through death he might destroy the one who has the power of death, that is, the devil, and deliver all those who through fear of death were subject to lifelong slavery (Hebrews 2:14-15).

The Son of God became one of us and experienced death for us so that He might thereby destroy the devil, the one who "has the power of death." That destruction of the devil that Jesus accomplished on the cross has unleashed divine power to liberate people who have lived their whole lives as slaves because they were afraid to die. Jesus faced death for sinners. This means that He became "a merciful and faithful high priest in the service of God, to make propitiation for the sins of the people" (Hebrews 2:17). Merciful, because he understands what it means to be haunted by death. Faithful, because having faced death, He did not sin but experienced it by entrusting Himself fully into the hands of His Father. Therefore, "because he himself has suffered when tempted, he is able to help those who are being tempted" (Hebrews 2:18).

Christians are not immune to the temptation to fear death and, therefore, to live their lives enslaved by this fear. Jesus can set us free from such fear and enable us to face frightening things with faith because He has defeated sin, death, and the devil in our behalf. We do not have to be paralyzed by the prospect of danger or death. Nor do we have to idolize safety. Jesus has defeated death and there is no safer place in the world than to be in Him through faith.

The new religion, teaching that you are god, cannot help but adopt the sacredness of safety. If you are god, then you certainly cannot let yourself die. But, if you are a creature made in God's image, indeed one redeemed by the blood of God Himself, then you are free to die well. You are *redeemed*. You have eternal life in Christ. You can say with the apostle Paul, "For to me to live is Christ, and to die is gain. If I am to live in the flesh, that means fruitful labor for me. Yet which I shall choose I cannot tell. I am hard pressed between the two. My desire is to depart and be with Christ, for that is far better" (Philippians 1:21-23).

David appeared to have this sense about him when he went to that Philistine battle line. Goliath bellowed his blasphemies, and the Israelites, along with Saul, were afraid. But, while those Israelite soldiers were not willing to face the danger, David was. He was not foolish. He was prepared. He had battled with beasts before. He was not, however, trusting in himself. He was looking to heavenly truth, which enabled him to follow his Lord in the face of Dagon worship and a severe threat to his life. He proclaimed truth to the giant:

> You come to me with a sword and with a spear and with a javelin, but I come to you in the name of the LORD of hosts, the God of the armies of Israel, whom you have defied. This day the LORD will deliver you into my hand, and I will strike you down and cut off your head. And I will give the dead bodies of the host of the Philistines this day to the birds of the air and

to the wild beasts of the earth, that all the earth may know that there is a God in Israel, and that all this assembly may know that the LORD saves not with sword and spear. For the battle is the LORD's, and he will give you into our hand (1 Samuel 17:45-47).

Our generation needs to know that there is a God in Israel. America needs to know that the Lord saves not with sword and spear. The battle belongs to Him.

Face the danger.

PART 3:

FOLLOWING JESUS IN ALL SPHERES

8

RAISE YOUR CHILDREN: EDUCATING THE NEXT GENERATION

When it comes to religion, there is no neutrality. You will have the Christian kind, or you will have some other kind. The culture in which we live is steeped in the other kind. It has a well-organized discipleship program. The question is not whether but which. It is not whether your children will practice a religion, but which religion they will practice. It is not whether they will learn to obey, but which law they will obey. It is not whether they will believe, but which gospel they will believe. It is not whether they will serve a god, but which god they will serve.

We must understand the times. It would be one thing to raise children in Israel's united kingdom under Solomon. The temple was glorious in that day. The songs rang out. The sacrifices sent up a continual aroma reminding Israel of sin and salvation. However, it would be another thing to raise children during the divided kingdom of Rehoboam and Jeroboam. Peculiar parental temptations would arise in that context. But, 21st century America is neither of those. We raise children in Babylon. We are in exile.

Some may claim that such a statement is fearmongering. But, consider what we do. We murder nearly a million children in their mother's womb every year. We have grown men throwing dollar bills at a scantily dressed young boy in a bar.[1] The government considers drafting women into the military.[2] We educate children in every single subject according to a philosophy that says there is no god. It is fair to say that we are in exile. In this exile, the next generation is being discipled in America's new religion.

If the first problem is parents not knowing we are in the ruins of a Christian civilization, the second problem is parents riddled with anxiety that this is the case. What parent has not thought, "I'm just going to pull down the shades, lock the doors, and keep little sweet Johnny safe from the big bad world?" But God does not call us to bite our fingernails in Babylon. He tells us to rebuild. The Bible refers to children as arrows (Psalm 127:4). Arrows are not made to stay in the quiver. They are made to do battle. A warrior's arrow has done its job when it lies bloody and shattered, having hit its mark. You cannot protect your children from false gospel by hiding them. You protect them from false gospel by giving them real gospel. Then, you send them out into the world to tear down strongholds.

---

1   Doug Mainwaring, "11-year-old 'drag kid' dances in popular NYC gay club as patrons toss money at him," Life Site, December 17, 2018, https://www.lifesitenews.com/news/11-year-old-drag-kid-dances-in-popular-nyc-gay-club-as-patrons-toss-money-a.

2   Sarah Mervosh and John Ismay, "Women Should Have to Register for Military Draft, Too, Commission Tells Congress," *The New York Times*, March 24, 2020, https://www.nytimes.com/2020/03/24/us/women-military-draft-selective-service.html.

The Catechetical Instruction of the New Religion

By and large, the government schools in America serve as the new religion's catechetical training system. The new faith involves a hardened secularism in which humanity is god. It preaches a false hope of universal equality and autonomy. These ideas undergird much of what goes on in American public education.

We certainly do not mean that everyone involved in government schoolwork is guilty of training up the next generation in an erroneous faith. We know many godly public school teachers and administrators. We should thank God for Christians working to see the present condition of our public schools improved. There is much work to be done. The trouble in the public school culture has not arrived overnight.

John Dewey was quite influential in American education. His work is often employed in training public educators. The problem is that his atheism found its way into his philosophy of education. He was an original signer of the 1933 Humanist Manifesto, which states,

> The time is past for mere revision of traditional attitudes. Science and economic change have disrupted the old beliefs. Religions the world over are under the necessity of coming to terms with new conditions created by a vastly increased knowledge and experience. In every field of human activity, the vital movement is now in the direction of a candid and explicit humanism. In order that religious humanism may be better understood we, the undersigned, desire to make certain affirmations which we believe the

facts of our contemporary life demonstrate... While this age does owe a vast debt to the traditional religions, it is none the less obvious that any religion that can hope to be a synthesizing and dynamic force for today must be shaped for the needs of this age.[3]

The very first affirmation of the Humanist Manifesto was, "Religious humanists regard the universe as self-existing and not created."[4] As we mentioned in a previous chapter, self-existence is a divine attribute. Theologians speak of it as an incommunicable attribute, namely an attribute not found in the creature. John Dewey affirmed that the universe maintains attributes of deity. Given his influence, it is no surprise that God is not honored as Creator in the education of American children in government schools.

The education system in America is thoroughly secular. We are not talking about the immorality in the schools. There is plenty of that. But, we refer to the precommitment to view any and all subjects of study as not belonging to God, to ignore or even deny that they exist and operate according to the Creator. We have bought into the falsehood that you can thoroughly teach the subject matter without considering the Creator and Sustainer of the subject matter.

It does not take long to discover the inevitable question a child will ask when analyzing given topics of study. When you examine the human body, you discover an intricate system, which operates in remarkable ways. You cannot look at the liver, the intestines, or the circulatory system without being confronted with order and design. Did the system

---

3 "Humanist Manifesto I," American Humanist Association: Good Without a God, accessed November 23, 2020, https://americanhumanist.org/what-is-humanism/manifesto1.

4 Ibid.

just come together on its own? Or is there a Designer? The student cannot escape that question, and the teacher cannot dodge that question. The same question presents itself in mathematics, history, art, and every other subject. To ignore the question is to answer it. Ignoring the question teaches that God is irrelevant to the subject matter.

We also face significant trouble with motivation without God. Lack of motivation is a universal problem. It is because of sin that we fall into laziness. But, the secularist has no divine impetus to employ. Teachers train whole students. They cannot say that motivation is not their department. Sadly, secular education supplies only secular stimuli. Greed, pride, and shame become key motivators in such a system.

Christians in general, and parents specifically, must reclaim their responsibility to raise up the next generation to know Christ and His world. The point is not only to teach. Indeed, parents need to teach their children the truth, whether it is found in natural or special revelation. But, we must do more than simply teach our children the Ten Commandments and the Apostle's Creed. When Paul tells fathers in Ephesians 6:4 to raise their children in the nurture and admonition of the Lord, he refers to an all-encompassing enculturating in Christ. To raise them as Paul instructs implies steeping them in the truth, goodness, and beauty of Christ and His ways.

COURAGEOUSLY RAISING THE NEXT GENERATION

Deuteronomy 6 displays a glorious vision for parents. Moses tells Israel that they are to do God's law, multiply, enter the Promised Land, and teach their children at all times and in various contexts (Deuteronomy 6:1-7). God's truth was to mark their very bodies, homes, doors, and gates (Deuteronomy 6:8-9). God's law and gospel related to their forefathers, cisterns, vineyards, olive trees, full bellies, past slavery, present enemies, and their future (Deuteronomy 6:9-12, 19, 24). Israel was marked by God's truth. His revelation thoroughly shaped their worldview. Their culture was God's law and promises. All of this was true as they entered the Promised Land to battle against the giants.

You cannot help but see the contrast. You cannot avoid noticing how such a culture is abandoned in our day. Many Christians in America have lost this worldview. Israel was to do God's law, but today to talk about doing God's law is to open yourself to the charge of being legalistic. Israel was to be fruitful and multiply, but today being fruitful in rearing children has been detached from fulfilling God's purposes in the world. Israel was to enter the land and possess it, but today Christianity is often lived abstractly and theoretically without application to vocation, tradition, education, and civil life. Israel was to teach their children at all times, but today life is structured to ensure parents have no time to do that teaching. Israel marked their bodies with God's truth, but today there are attempts to mark ourselves with our transgressions. Israel's homes were set apart by God's standards, but our home life has blended in with the world's prerogatives.

We've lost our appreciation for our forefathers in the faith. We drink from cisterns and eat with full bellies, but do so without thanksgiving because we do not know to whom we should offer our gratitude. In our Babylon, oranges just grow on trees. Bananas just sprout forth of their own accord. Cows just have more cows so you can enjoy steak. Do not ask why cows beget cows. Do not worry about the Creator who keeps meeting that desire in your belly by making chickens have more chickens. We do not talk about *Him* in Babylon.

Because God's truth marked them, Israel knew their enemies (Deuteronomy 6:19). But there is increasing confusion in our day concerning who are the good guys and who are the bad guys. Israel understood their past and future in light of God's law and gospel. But the rising generation is brought up storyless. All is a blank piece of paper for them. They are encouraged to write their own story rather than play their part in God's.

If we would raise our children amid the rise of America's new religion, then there are several things we must do.

FEAR GOD

First, we must fear God. The Bible refers to fearing the Lord at least 150 times. Moses knew how fundamental this was to the work of parenting. He instructed, "Now this is the commandment—the statutes and the rules—that the LORD your God commanded me to teach you, that you may do them in the land to which you are going over, to possess it, that you may fear the LORD your God, you and your son and your son's son" (Deuteronomy 6:1).

Israel was to fear the Lord from generation to generation. They were not merely to hand down God's commandments. They indeed had to do that much. But there was an important goal attached to the handing down of those commandments. They were to pass down those statutes so that their children and grandchildren would fear God. So it is today. When we talk of educating the next generation, that includes education in the fear of the Lord. The fear of the Lord is an integral ingredient to any education. How could it not be?—"The fear of the LORD is the beginning of knowledge" (Proverbs 1:7). And, "The fear of the Lord is the beginning of wisdom; all those who practice it have a good understanding. His praise endures forever!" (Psalm 111:10).

Parents cannot raise their children in something to which they themselves are not committed. If we would raise up a generation as God intends, then we must reverence the God who is. He is an awesome God. He dwells in unapproachable light (1 Timothy 6:16). He is a consuming fire (Hebrews 12:29). He makes mountains smoke (Psalm 104:32). He makes the waters divide. He created man from the dust. He gives life and breath to every living thing. And He has condescended to speak to us. If we do not fear God, then we cannot raise a generation to fear Him.

The fear of the Lord involves a right understanding and use of His law. If we do not fear God, then we will distort the function of His law. One of the uses of God's law is that it drives us to Christ. We should teach our children God's law in the fear of the Lord so they might see their desperate need for Christ. But, if we attempt to teach God's law without fearing Him, our teaching becomes mere rule-keeping. The law, which should arrest them and reveal their sinfulness, will be presented in a distorted fashion.

Without the fear of God, God's standard becomes arbitrary and legalistic. Geerhardus Vos expressed well how an unusual form of legalism can creep in if we lose a sense of esteem for God—"Legalism is a peculiar kind of submission to God's law, something that no longer feels the personal divine touch in the rule it submits to."[5] Along the same lines,

5 Geerhardus Vos, *The Self Disclosure of Jesus,* ed. and rev. J. G. Vos (1926; repr. Nutley, NJ: Presbyterian & Reformed, 1953).

Sinclair Ferguson has said, "Legalism is simply separating the law of God from the person of God."[6]

The new religion suffers from just this mistake. The rules and regulations of the hardened secularism permeating our times do not come with a living, Spirit-wrought relationship with the law-giver. As with many other false religions, the way toward acceptance in the new faith is through law-keeping. But, Christianity teaches that the way to acceptance is through the law-keeping of the Son of God. Fallen people cannot measure up. We need a Savior. By grace, through faith, sinners come into genuine relationship with their Creator. In that blood-bought fellowship with God, Christians take God at His Word, following His commands. Parents must remember this gospel. They will then cultivate homes in which God is known and loved, and His standard is known and loved.

If we lack the fear of God, we will see His gospel as lukewarm at best and therapeutic folly at worst. There is no place for a bloody cross without the fear of God. What place has the shedding of blood if man is not sinful? Who needs a mediator if there is no chasm between God and man? Certain sectors of American evangelicalism have heard much about the cross but very little about the fear of the Lord. The cross has now become a senseless instrument of death that they are in danger of discarding. Man has been elevated to a place he does not belong, tracking with the new religion's teaching. God has been lowered, fashioned by false teaching to be altogether like us. With an elevated man and lowered deity, there is no longer a need for the perfect God-man, Jesus. Without the fear of God, some are discovering that you can simply dispense with justification by faith.

---

6   Sinclair Ferguson, *The Whole Christ* (Wheaton, IL: Crossway, 2016), 83.

The next generation, then, must be educated in the fear of the Lord.

POSSESS THE LAND

If we would raise our children in these increasingly secular times, then we must possess the land. The land plays a prominent part in both the Old and New Testaments. Moses said God told him to teach His statutes that Israel might possess the land (Deuteronomy 6:1, 18, 23). This land would flow with milk and honey (Deuteronomy 6:3). God would bring them into that Promised Land (Deuteronomy 6:10).

While in the New Covenant, we are not looking to secure the physical land of Canaan, it is still true that the earth is the Lord's (Psalm 24:1). Jesus indeed has all authority in heaven and on earth (Matthew 28:18). Jesus taught us to pray that His kingdom would come and His will would be done on earth (Matthew 6:10). Jesus shall surely have the nations as His heritage and the ends of the earth as His possession (Psalm 2:8). These things being true, we must train the coming generation to follow Jesus with their feet firmly planted right here on the ground. Far too many Christians live disjointed lives. They maintain a theoretical commitment to Christ but lack faith and obedience in real-time. The aim is not merely to get our children to believe an idea or adopt our set of principles. It is instead to train them to believe and obey the King of the world.

We and our children are facing an ever-increasing attempt to unrealize our Christianity. You can have it, the world says, but only in imaginary form. You can do whatever you want within your own four walls. But do not bring your faith out here into the public square. It became common only a few years ago to speak of freedom of worship rather than freedom of religion. You are free to pray. But, you may not enter civic life while exercising your religion. This presupposition undergirds our secular age. But our children, like ourselves, have to follow Jesus at all times and in all places. We do so in marriage, vocation, education, military service, recreation, financial exchanges, and political decisions.

If our nation's current trajectory holds, then our children and grandchildren will face earthly challenges in ways that we have not. New ethical questions will present themselves. New opportunities for courage and sacrifice are upon us already. But the troubling thing is, in many ways, a defeatist mentality has already been cultivated in a large swath of evangelical Christians. We have thought that Jesus is losing the battle on earth, and now our increasingly sinful culture seemingly proves our unbelief. With such an outlook, we will fail to train the coming generation to live for Christ in the world.

We recall a time when missionaries dreamed about changing the very landscape of civilization through the proclamation of God's Word. They wanted mosques replaced with chapels and minarets replaced with steeples. Paul and the other apostles made such a stir that people said, "these men have turned the world upside down" (Acts 17:6)! Our forefathers in the faith lived on the earth for Christ so as, at times, to shut down the very industry of idol making (Acts 19:27).

If our children would follow Jesus amid America's new religion, then they must know that "the earth is the LORD's and the fullness thereof, the world and those who dwell therein, for he has founded it upon the seas and established it upon the rivers" (Psalm 24:1). As Abraham Kuyper has said, "There is not a square inch in the whole domain of our human existence over which Christ, who is Sovereign over all, does not cry, 'Mine!'"[7]

REJECT IDOLS

Training the next generation involves equipping them to reject idols. Moses warned Israel that they must not forget the Lord once they entered the land, enjoying their homes and vineyards. He directed, "You shall not go after other gods, the gods of the peoples who are around you" (Deuteronomy 6:14). Israel, nevertheless, did just that. They were Canaanized. Eventually, they wanted a king like the nations around them rather than a God-fearing one (1 Samuel 8:20). We must learn from their errors.

The apostle John concludes his first letter with this stark admonition, "Little children, keep yourselves from idols" (1 John 5:21). If we are going to do this, then we must learn to see them. Doing so comes with its challenges. The false religion among us is subtle and deceptive. It masquerades as if it were no religion. The Canaanites, for example, plainly stated that they killed their children in worship of Molech. Israel had the advantage of things being a bit clearer. However, the false religion in our midst does not openly admit that the bloody work done at Planned Parenthood is actually child sacrifice to the god of self. Regrettably, the Christian community has bought into much of the terminology and worldview of secularism, leaving us unable to identify and reject the idolatry.

---

7 Abraham Kuyper, *Abraham Kuyper: A Centennial Reader*, ed. James D. *Bratt* (Grand Rapids: Eerdmans, 1998), 488.

The second commandment says,

> You shall not make for yourself a carved image, or any likeness of anything that is in heaven above, or that is in the earth beneath, or that is in the water under the earth. You shall not bow down to them or serve them, for I the LORD your God am a jealous God, visiting the iniquity of the fathers on the children to the third and the fourth generation of those who hate me, but showing steadfast love to thousands of those who love me and keep my commandments (Deuteronomy 20:4-6).

This commandment not only forbids crafting an image by which one attempts to worship the true God. It also prohibits the worship and service of false deities. When answering the question of what is forbidden in the second commandment, the Westminster Larger Catechism states, "the making of any representation of feigned deities, and all worship of them, or service belonging to them."[8] Feigned deities include the human self. So the rising generation must learn that man is not the measure of all things. They need to be trained in the difference between the image of God and God Himself.

One reason we are not better at rejecting idols is because we have lost a sense of God's character. He is a jealous God. His jealousy is supplied as a reason annexed to the second commandment. God is fervently zealous for His own worship. Modern ears consider such a notion unbefitting, for we have forgotten that "God is not a man" (Numbers 23:19). Should He be a mere man, then visiting the father's iniquity upon his children and grandchildren would not be a virtue. But,

---

8 "Westminster Larger Catechism," Orthodox Presbyterian Church, Q:109. accessed December 12, 2020, https://opc.org/lc.html.

God's holiness and perfection teach us that "his revengeful indignation against all false worship"[9] is entirely good and just.

Not only have we lost a sense of God's jealousy, but we have also abandoned a perception of His abounding grace. The reason given for obedience to the second commandment was not only that God visits the father's iniquity on the children to the third and fourth generation. Moses also says that God shows steadfast love to *thousands* of those who love Him. Hating Him gets trouble to a few generations. Loving Him results in steadfast love to thousands. Our God is generous. His gospel is really good news. When we grasp His amazing grace, we will reject idols, hating false worship as He hates false worship.

False gods cannot compare to the true God. Isaiah said it well, "Who fashions a god or casts an idol that is profitable for nothing? Behold, all his companions shall be put to shame, and the craftsmen are only human. Let them all assemble, let them stand forth. They shall be terrified; they shall be put to shame together" (Isaiah 44:10-11). What a silly thing it is to believe in ourselves. Very often, we cannot even find a matching pair of socks. What kind of life do you expect to live if you trust in a guy who cannot find a matching pair of socks? Here is the education our children need: "Why O children would you want to grow up to be whatever you want when you could grow up to be what God wants? Why would you want to follow your heart when you could instead follow Christ?"

---

9 Ibid, Q:110.

REMEMBER EXODUS

Courageously raising children in the Lord's discipline and instruction requires fearing God, possessing the land, rejecting idols, and finally, remembering the Exodus. Moses knew that Israel's God-given traditions and statutes would spark questions in the children. He says, "When your son asks you in time to come, 'What is the meaning of the testimonies and the statutes and the rules that the LORD our God has commanded you?' then you shall say to your son, 'We were Pharaoh's slaves in Egypt. And the LORD brought us out of Egypt with a mighty hand'" (Deuteronomy 6:20).

Our children will have the same questions. "Why do you do all these things, dad? Why do we gather with God's people every Sunday? Why do we sing? Why do you catechize me? Why does mom speak respectfully to you? Why do you not have two wives? Why do we open our home to the needy? Why do I see you honor grandpa and grandma? Why do you discipline me when I tell lies? What is all of this about?"

The response is: Oh, my son, because God brought us out of Egypt with a mighty hand. We were slaves there, stuck in our sin. But God told the one who tyrannized us to let us go, and God took us away. His Son paid the price for us, and all of our old ways died with Him. God's Son has been raised, and we have been raised in Him to live this new life, fearing God, living wisely in His world, rejecting idols, and glorying in His gospel.

We live this way, son, because our God redeems through His Son Jesus Christ. Believe His gospel always. Be diligent in keeping His commands. As I have feared Him, you fear Him. As you have seen me live out His ways in all of life, so you follow me as I follow Christ. Follow the way I have pointed out falsehood. Reject lies. Do not be taken captive by vain philosophies. And son, do not ever forget the Exodus. Forget not when the Lamb was slain. That Lamb has risen again. His name is Jesus, and He saves from sin. You have seen me fail. You know I am not god. And you are not either. Our world elevates humanity to the place of deity. But, there is only one Christ, and we are not Him—"there is salvation in no one else, for there is no other name under heaven given among men by which we must be saved" (Acts 4:12).

9

GO TO CHURCH: ASSEMBLING TO WORSHIP ACCORDING TO GOD'S WORD

The assembly of the saints is essential to following Jesus. The author of Hebrews exhorts, "And let us consider how to stir up one another to love and good works, not neglecting to meet together, as is the habit of some, but encouraging one another, and all the more as you see the Day drawing near" (Hebrews 10:24-25). We experience normal days and unusual days. We live through standard years and peculiarly challenging ones. Average times come, and particularly evil times come. The apostle Paul urges us to "stand in the evil day" (Ephesians 6:13). If you must go to church in common times, how much more must you do so as America's secularism metastasizes?

GOD'S WORD: PUBLICLY ANNOUNCED IN CORPORATE ASSEMBLY

Significant challenges confront the assembly of the saints. We saw increasing challenges in the year 2020. The two surface-level impediments to church assembly were concern over the COVID virus and governmental prohibitions of church gatherings. But the virus and despotic governors were not the only hindrances to the church meeting. The church was, in many ways, primed for compromising public assembly by a malnourished understanding of the church and public worship.

We have forsaken the truth that, in our worship assemblies, we testify of heavenly realities to a lost and dying world. Corporate worship has become a thing primarily for the individual. We go to church to "get fed." Unquestionably, Christians are edified by the corporate worship of our Lord. Indeed, one design of such an assembly is to strengthen the individual. But, much more is involved in the public worship of the Creator.

We need a recovery of the vertical testimony of the church. There is a reason why many churches have those steeples soaring toward the sky. Humanity must be reminded that there is a God in heaven. If the church does not assemble, then that corporate witness vanishes. The 1689 confession conveys that public worship is a foundational purpose of the church:

> In the execution of this power wherewith he is so intrusted, the Lord Jesus calleth out of the world unto himself, through the ministry of his word, by his Spirit, those that are given unto him by his Father, that they may walk before him in all the ways of obedience, which he prescribeth to them in his word. Those thus called, he commandeth to walk together in particular societies, or churches, for their mutual edification, and *the due performance of that public worship*, which he requireth of them in the world.[1]

---

1 The Baptist Confession of Faith 1689 (Carlisle, PA: Banner of Truth, 2012), 26:5 (emphasis ours).

Jerusalem was a city that testified to the glory of God on earth. Many kings tried to snuff out Israel's witness, prohibiting the people from ascending to Mount Zion to sing the psalms of God. In Nehemiah's day, the enemies of God attempted to stop the rebuilding of that city. Sanballat and Geshem sought to end Nehemiah's rebuilding project. But Nehemiah had other plans, saying, "I am doing a great work and I cannot come down" (Nehemiah 6:3). We have already heard that it was out of that city God sent forth His truth into the world (Psalm 110:2; Acts 1:8).

Christians in America must see that we, too, are doing a good work and cannot come down from our public assemblies. When we assemble, we ascend to the sacred gathering where we testify to God's truth. In Ephesians 3:10 Paul states that it is "through the church [that] the manifold wisdom of God might now be made known to the rulers and authorities in the heavenly places." As a church lives together, serves together, evangelizes together, and worships together, God's multifaceted wisdom is put on display to unseen principalities and powers. Every church is bearing such a testimony every time they meet together for worship as the Lord teaches us to do. When a church gathers for worship in this way God is glorified, the membership is edified, and the world—both seen and unseen—is given another demonstration that Jesus Christ is Lord.

The new religion seeks to snuff out this public witness, just like Sanballat and Geshem from many years ago. But, with the psalmist, we say, "I was glad when they said to me, 'Let us go to the house of the Lord'" (Psalm 122:1)!

GOD'S WORD: WHY CHURCHES ASSEMBLE

We do not only announce God's Word when assembling as churches. God's Word is also the basis for our assembly. God has said to assemble. How could we not? God worked six days in creation and rested on the seventh. He calls His people to follow His pattern (Exodus 20:8-11). The 1689 confession states,

> As it is the law of nature, that in general a proportion of time, by God's appointment, be set apart for the worship of God, so by his Word, in a positive moral, and perpetual commandment, binding all men, in all ages, he hath particularly appointed one day in seven for a sabbath to be kept holy unto him, which from the beginning of the world to the resurrection of Christ was the last day of the week, and from the resurrection of Christ was changed into the first day of the week, which is called the Lord's day: and is to be continued to the end of the world as the Christian Sabbath, the observation of the last day of the week being abolished.[2]

Under the Old Covenant, the sabbath involved resting and worshiping on the seventh day of the week. Under the New Covenant, with the resurrection of Christ on the first day of the week, the pattern was kept, but the day changed (John 20:1; Revelation 1:10; 1 Corinthians 16:2).

On the Lord's Day, Christians set aside one day in seven to worship Almighty God. Many consider the fourth commandment to be a burden unfit for New Covenant people. But, the fourth commandment is in keeping with the eternal

---

2 The Baptist Confession of Faith 1689, 22:7.

character of our holy God. Our day of rest is not a drudgery but a delight.

Our persecuted brothers and sisters in China have demonstrated a far greater love for gathered worship than we do in America. In 2018-19, the Chinese government cracked down on Christians.[3] Pastor Wang Yi of the Early Rain Covenant Church was, along with more than one hundred of his fellow members, arrested, harassed, and worse. Pastor Yi prepared written documents in advance of the persecution he saw coming. He wanted to make sure his church would be properly instructed about how to think and react to persecution if he were no longer available to teach them.

He wrote an article called "14 Decisions: In the Face of Persecution, What Will I Do?" The very first decision is:

> **Do not stop gathering together:** Under no circumstances will we stop or give up on gathering publicly, especially the corporate worship of believers on Sunday. God's sovereignty is higher than any secular authority and the church's mission and the Bible's teaching on not neglecting to gather together is higher than any secular law. Regardless of whether the Religious Affairs Bureau and the police take administrative and forceful measures toward Sunday worship, whether or not their enforcement follows due process, I will resist by peaceful means. I will not cooperate with the police banning, shutting down, dissolving, or sealing up the church and its gathering.

---

3 Western China Presbytery, "Letter to All Christian Churches to Pray for Early Rain Covenant Church in Chengdu," *China Partnership* (blog), December 14, 2018, https://www.chinapartnership.org/blog/2018/12/letter-for-all-christian-churches-to-pray-for-early-rain-covenant-church-in-chengdu.

I will not stop convening, hosting and participating
in the church's public worship, until the police seizes
my personal freedom by force.4

Our Chinese brothers refuse to give up under persecution
what so many American Christians voluntarily neglect or
dismiss under ease. Could it be that we have enjoyed gospel
privileges for so long that we have taken them for granted?
Could it be that we have affirmed the authority of God's
Word for so long that we have come to assume that we are
submitted to it when in reality, we do not think much about
it at all?

In general, modern evangelicals are not in any danger of
rejecting the authority of Scripture out of hand. Our danger
is losing the authority of Scripture by assuming that we are
submissive to it when we go following our own whims. May
God deliver us from such a deadly mistake. That mistake
involves being taken captive by hollow and deceptive philosophy (Colossians 2:8).

GOD'S WORD OVER MAN'S MIND

God's Word is announced by the church and grounds the
very assembly of churches. It also serves to keep human reason and wisdom in its place as churches assemble to worship.
The new religion exalts human reason. We, also, can easily
fall into the sin of high-mindedness, elevating human reason
over revelation. The church in America has not maintained
a clear conviction that divine revelation trumps human
reason. So we were sitting ducks when the governmental

---

4 Wang Yi, "Wang Yi's 14 Decisions: In the Face of Persecution, What
Will I Do?" China Partnership, December 17, 2018. https://www.china-
partnership.org/blog/2018/12/in-the-face-of-persecution-what-will-i-do.

overreach occurred in 2020, prohibiting many churches from gathering.

Jonathan Edwards, the great New England pastor and theologian, articulated it well when he said, "The judge, and the rule by which he judges, are diverse."[5] By "judge" and "rule," he referred respectively to reason and revelation. In his day, Edwards lamented that some sought to elevate reason to a place where it did not belong. Reason is only the judge. It serves you well as *the faculty* by which you understand truth. But, reason is not *the rule* by which you judge. The difference between *the rule* and *the faculty* is a world of difference. The *rule* by which you judge is not reason but revelation.

We suspect that much of our evangelical leadership is confused at the following points: They agree that divine revelation—whether general or special—is indeed the rule by which Christians should judge religious things. They also agree that revelation is the rule by which the church should judge church things. They do not, however, believe that revelation is the rule by which man is to judge all things. If life were a pizza, they believe most of the slices fall under divine revelation. But, certain slices—the political, civil, or sociological—fall under another standard.

We have seen this confusion in the response to a very public showdown between Grace Community Church (where John MacArthur pastors) and the California State Governor Gavin Newsom. Some evangelical Christians (including prominent leaders) maintained that pastor MacArthur had no higher standard to which he could appeal, given that the governor had mandated no indoor worship services. Neither

---

5 Jonathan Edwards, "Medium of Moral Government," in *The Works of Jonathan Edwards* (Peadbody, MA: Hendrickson, 2006), Volume 2, 489.

did governor Newsom have to ground his mandate in divine revelation—human reason would suffice. The matter of COVID shutdowns was not inherently religious, this line of reasoning concluded. So divine revelation did not speak to it. The mind of the governor had spoken, and Christians should dutifully comply out of love for their neighbors and government officials.

However, the truth is that both Pastor MacArthur and Governor Newsom must appeal to the rule (divine revelation) and, with their faculty (reason), determine what ought to be done. If governor Newsom is not to judge truth by divine revelation, what standard is he to use? Should he determine the actual state of things by appealing to his own thought? Should the people's will be the final standard by which he comes to know the nature of reality? In the words of the apostle Paul, "By no means" (Romans 6:2)! Governor Newsom is a servant of Jesus and, therefore, must do what Jesus says (Romans 13:4).

The more pressing question, however, is: Why are we American Christians just realizing this now? It seems some of the secular humanism our fathers warned us about has worked its way into our thinking. Edwards was not the only one to fight the faulty exaltation of reason. Charles Spurgeon warned, "the new religion practically sets 'thought' above revelation, and, constitutes man the supreme judge of what ought to be true."[6] Thought above revelation was the spirit of the age. That spirit was present outside the church and found its way into the church. We are naive to think we can let revelation be subordinated to "thought" out there and not end up with the same thing *in the church*.

---

6 Iain Murray, *The Forgotten Spurgeon* (Carlisle, PA: Banner of Truth, 2017), 198.

We are confident that thoughtful Christians repudiate reason over revelation when it comes to what they deem sacred things. But, many of those same Christians conceive of an area of life, or the world, where reason reigns, not revelation. We have bifurcated God's world. Christian *practice* has been put into a box, a lane. We ought not to let that happen. If we do, it is nothing other than a dereliction of Christian duty.

Suppose reason is the final standard in California civil life. In that case, Pastor John MacArthur was wrong, perhaps a bit cranky, and should have just gone along with the governor's mandate even if he disagreed. After all, it is only one man's reason against another's, and the governor is the civil leader. If reason is the final standard in California civil life, then Governor Newsom had no obligation to consider Scripture, pray for wisdom from above, or listen to what Jesus says through creation and providence. But if revelation is the final standard, then Pastor MacArthur was obligated to determine whether the governor's mandate was in keeping with the job assignment that Jesus has given civil magistrates (Romans 13).

Similarly, if revelation is the final standard, then Governor Newsom was obligated to look to what Jesus requires of him as a civil magistrate. He should have considered what God has revealed about the virus as well. He needed to observe what God has said about the nature and necessity of Christian worship. His duty involved humbly and prayerfully seeking God's revealed wisdom on the matter so that he could determine what is involved in prohibiting church worship.

As long as we live in the bifurcation—failing to see that revelation is the ultimate authority for all people, in all places, at all times—we will be unable to live faithfully. Examples abound, but one is that our intercession for civil authorities will fall flat. God requires that intercessions be made for "kings and all who are in high positions" (1 Timothy 2:2). And yet, according to the fractured worldview that claims a sacred realm governed by revelation and a secular realm governed by reason, what are we to pray for Governor Newsom? *"God, make him smarter? Please, Lord, make him fairer?"* Fair according to what standard? How will Governor Newsom get smarter, if not by looking to divine revelation, the final standard of all truth?

When Christians assemble to worship God through His Word, they are reminded of their limitations. God is the One adored, not us. We go through a weekly reminder that we are finite. We discover every Lord's Day that we have little pea brains compared to God's infinite knowledge and wisdom. We do not worship Him based on human reason but on the basis of His perfect Word. We hear His Word, sing His Word, pray His Word, read His Word, and even dramatize His Word in the Lord's Supper and Baptism. The new religion, teaching that man is God, claims human reason as the final standard. Yet, the assembly of the saints for worship proclaims just the opposite. God is God. His inspired Word is the final standard.

God's Word Directs Church Worship

It is not hard to find examples of churches neglecting Scripture in an attempt to spice up their worship gatherings. A Florida pastor once hired a stunt man to help him sit in a car while it was blown up on the church parking lot. After the smoke cleared, he emerged unscathed. This feat was during a sermon series he was preaching on doing the impossible. And Pastor Lawrence Bishop II of Solid Rock Church in Monroe,

Ohio, calls himself the "cowboy pastor."[7] He once rode a bull during a worship service. After about three seconds, he was bucked off, then climbed onto the platform and began to preach.

Obviously, these are extreme examples, but they reflect an evangelical church culture that is at best confused and at worst clueless regarding the whole question of what corporate worship ought to be. What a church does on Sunday morning is very often more influenced by Hollywood, Madison Avenue, sociology, or psychology than by the Bible.[8]

In many ways, we find ourselves in a situation similar to that which the Protestant Reformers faced. As Sinclair Ferguson notes,

> The sixteenth-century Reformers shared a deep, underlying concern that late medieval worship had become a kind of spectator event. The congregation was largely passive. "Worshipers," if they could be thus described, were essentially observers of the drama of the Mass, and listeners to the words of the choir. The service of divine worship was an event in which the congregants were not participants so much as spectators... Worship was, for all practical purposes, done for you—vicariously.[9]

---

7 Carol Kuruvilla, "6 of the Most Ridiculous Stunts Pastors Have Pulled To Get People To Church," HuffPost, May 24, 2015, https://www.huffpost.com/entry/pastor-stunts-church_n_7346314.

8 For more examples see Tom Ascol, "Interesting Times and Changing Times in the SBC," Founders Ministries, accessed November 26, 2020, https://founders.org/2020/02/17/interesting-times-and-changing-times-in-the-sbc.

9 Sinclair Ferguson, *Reformation Worship* (Greensboro, NC: New Growth Press, 2018), xvii.

Much of the worship in our modern churches is similarly performance driven. What happens on the stage is given far more thought, planning, and care than what happens in the congregation. Faulty worship erodes Christian teaching and living. As John Calvin argued, the doctrine of salvation and the doctrine of worship go hand-in-hand. God acts in grace and power and we respond in faith and humility. These two truths undergird all of true Christianity.[10]

God cares about worship. He graphically demonstrated this when He killed Nadab and Abihu for offering strange fire on His altar in Leviticus 10. He has further expressed His concerns by addressing issues related to worship in the first four of the Ten Commandments. The importance of worship is conspicuous in the Old Testament with its detailed and complex prescriptions and procedures for approaching God. No one can catalog the Old Testament ritualistic and ceremonial requirements for worship without recognizing that God cares about how His people come before Him.

In the New Testament, we find Old Testament shadows and symbols giving way to the reality of Christ, which they anticipated. Because of the comparative lack of detailed prescriptions in the New Testament, one might be tempted to think that worship is less important now or that God is less concerned about how He is worshiped. But that is a terrible mistake which we must not make. Both Jesus and His apostles give us essential principles that must govern the corporate worship of God's people under the New Covenant. If churches would sustain the worship of God amid the rise of America's new religion, then we must be willing to mine these principles and apply them to our worship.

---

10   Ibid, vvi.

In John 4:24, Jesus said, "God is spirit, and those who worship him must worship in spirit and truth." Our worship involves submission to the Creator, a thing that the new religion forbids. J. I. Packer has explained,

> Worship in the Bible is the due response of rational creatures to the self-revelation of their Creator. It is an honoring and glorifying of God by gratefully offering back to Him all the good gifts, and all the knowledge of His greatness and graciousness, that He has given. It involves praising Him for what He is, thanking Him for what He has done, desiring Him to get Himself more glory by further acts of mercy, judgment, and power, and trusting Him with our concern for our own and others' future well-being.[11]

In a broad sense, all of life is worship. Paul says, "So, whether you eat or drink, or whatever you do, do all to the glory of God (1 Corinthians 10:31). In another place, he says, "I appeal to you therefore, brothers, by the mercies of God, to present your bodies as a living sacrifice, holy and acceptable to God, which is your spiritual worship" (Romans 12:1). In this sense, worship encompasses all of a Christian's life, where everything is to be carried out "Coram Deo," before the face of God in reverent submission.

In a narrower sense, the church assembles weekly to perform corporate worship according to God's truth. Jesus prayed to the Father, "Your Word is truth" (John 17:17). If we are going to worship "in truth," then we must learn to recognize the authority of Scripture in our worship. That authority includes Scripture regulating our worship. Some have sought to maintain a normative principle of worship

---

11 J. I. Packer, *Concise Theology* (Wheaton, IL: Tyndale, 1993), 98.

rather than a regulative principle. The normative principle teaches that whatever is not expressly forbidden in Scripture is allowed in worship. On the other hand, the regulative principle teaches that we may only worship God according to what He has prescribed in His Word. When we consider what we should do in worship the regulative principle asks, "Why?" The normative principle asks, "Why not?"

The regulative principle appears in the 1689 Confession when it says,

> But the acceptable way of worshipping the true God, is instituted by himself, and so limited by his own revealed will, that he may not be worshipped according to the imagination and devices of men, nor the suggestions of Satan, under any visible representations, or any other way not prescribed in the Holy Scriptures.[12]

The confession expounds the teaching of Christ in John 4. Worship that is not regulated by God's Word is not worship "in truth" and thus rejected by God. We ought not to be surprised or offended that God rejects worship that is not regulated by Scripture. Jesus rejected Samaritan worship: "you worship what you do not know" (John 4:22). Jesus rejected Pharisees' worship: "in vain do they worship me, teaching as doctrines the commandments of men" (Mark 7:7). There are numerous examples in the Old Testament of God rejecting worship (Exodus 32; Leviticus 10; 1 Samuel 15:22).

Undeniably, God cares about the way His people approach Him in worship. That is why He gave us the second commandment—not to make any carved images. It is the height of presumption to think that we can worship God in any old

---

12 *The* Baptist Confession of Faith 1689, 22:1.

way or by doing anything we want to when we gather with the people of God.

Imagine that you had known someone for forty years and wanted to honor him out of love and devotion. So you decided to host a banquet in his honor. You encourage everyone to come and spare no expense on decorations and the meal. You hire an interior designer to decorate the room in burnt orange and white. Then you hire a caterer to prepare an exquisite meal of codfish and caviar, with sweet potatoes, sauerkraut, and coconut cream pie for dessert. That kind of effort is going to cost you a great deal. And it will be an awe-inspiring display. But do you know what? The man you want to honor hates codfish, caviar, sweet potatoes, and burnt orange! If you want to honor someone, then you find out what he likes. Churches must learn to ask the question, "What does God want in worship?" They must then be guided into the Word to see what God has revealed about His desires on this subject. As they do so, they will pursue worship that is regulated by the Word.

If we are to follow Jesus amid America's increasing godlessness, then we must assemble with the saints according to His truth. We proclaim His truth in our churches. We cannot neglect that responsibility. We meet because He has told us to do so. We have no right to forsake sacred assembly. We are inoculated against the high-mindedness of the new religion as we assemble, hearing God's revelation proclaimed. And our very worship is directed and governed by God's Word. As we gather for the public worship of God, we will be edified and Christ will be magnified in heaven and on earth.

10

TEACH KINGS:
EXHORTING CIVIL AUTHORITIES
TO KISS THE SON

Christianity and America's new religion maintain two ir-reconcilable worldviews. The new religion teaches that the world is flat, egalitarian, a place in which there is no gradation of authority. Christianity teaches that the world is hierar-chical, with spheres in which God has established authority and order. In the former worldview, any attempt to exercise authority is domineering and any attempt to teach someone is an encroachment upon the exalted human self. You can, of course, exercise authority and teach if the autonomous individual permits you do so. But no authority is genuine, according to the new religion, unless the individual says so. On the other hand, the Christian worldview acknowledges the legitimacy of authority, for God establishes it. Authority must be exercised according to His instruction. When done so, such authority is legitimate. When not done so, it is illegitimate.

God has not only established authority in the home and church, but also in the civil realm. His design includes di-vinely-regulated positions of civil authority that come with great responsibility. Civil order and hierarchy accords with what we see in God's creation. We observe order and authority in the heavenly realm. God is the Most High with all authority. He has the authority to cast people into hell (Luke 12:5). He made all heavenly thrones and earthly authorities (Colossians 1:16). The devil is called a power (Ephesians 2:2). Christ disarmed heavenly powers (Colossians 1:15). Christians now wrestle against rulers and authorities in the heavenly places (Ephesians 6:12). We also see this order in the animal and plant kingdoms. The V-formation of the flight of birds exhibits order. The predator and prey relationship does so as well. In many animal groups, you find some form of hierarchy with a leader at the top. When scientists consider the natural world, they often classify their findings in parent/daughter terminology, observing priority and direction to the world.

When it comes to the nature and function of civil authority, it is not surprising that Christianity and America's new religion are in great conflict. The new religion has no basis for civil rule. The concept of civil authority itself is at odds with the new religion's presuppositions. Christians know that civil authority tracks with the nature of God, man, and the world. God has not been silent on how civil authority is to work. We cannot be silent either.

The church in America has fallen into two mistakes when it comes to the realm of civil magistrates. On the one hand, the church has simply been silent. We have pulled back from public life, leaving politics to the neo-pagans. In the name of spirituality, we have fallen into a form of pietism that has abandoned loving people in the world God made through promoting wise civil government. On the other hand, the church has engaged in manipulating and coercing kings rather than teaching them. We have fallen into the materialistic and mechanistic worldview of our times, assuming the only way to get the job done is by means prohibited in God's Word. Christians in this category see the errors of the widespread pietism. They claim to seek their fellow citizens' welfare through political work, and many of them are very well-intentioned. But modern Christian teaching has not supplied enough instruction to the dynamics of our civil life. Pastors have left those engaging in the political sphere with far too little truth, and they often fall into the temptation of adopting the methods of unbelievers. Those methods, arising from reliance on human wisdom, include partisan slander, bogus ballot harvesting, and various forms of manipulation.

If we would teach kings, then we must know who they serve.

KINGS SERVE THE KING OF KINGS

The year of our Lord 2020 bestowed many gifts on American citizens that we would prefer to return. But, through the rioting, looting, moral posturing, and over-reaching governors, God granted us the opportunity to check up on a *foundational* doctrine—the Christian doctrine that Jesus is King of Kings. Jesus is not merely *a* king. He is *the* King. He is not merely King of the church. He is not only King of heaven. He is King of body and soul, blood and dirt, Nancy Pelosi and Joe Biden, Mike Pence and Donald Trump.

The apostle Paul teaches that Jesus is the King over civil authorities when he writes, "the authorities are ministers of God" (Romans 13:6). God is the one who put them in office (Romans 13:1). They are His servants (Romans 13:4). Paul is not speaking of a vague deist god when he writes his letter to the Romans. He is talking about the God of the Bible, the tri-une God. He is saying that your city council ultimately serves Jesus. We do not get to take a vote on what the American people think when they refer to "one nation under God" and then import *that* notion of God back into what Paul meant.

If civil authorities are ministers of Christ, it follows that they must do what Christ says. While they are responsible to obey Christ as individuals, they are particularly accountable to execute their public office how Christ would have them. Now, this does not mean at all that they are to legislate church attendance. They have a lane in which to operate and that lane does not include ecclesiastical matters. Nevertheless, being ministers of Christ means their legislation is regulated by Christ. They have no authority to disobey the One from whom they receive authority—"For there is no authority except from God, and those that exist have been instituted by God" (Romans 13:1). Human rulers are not free to rebel against their King—"They will make war on the Lamb, and the Lamb will conquer them, for he is Lord of lords and King of kings" (Revelation 17:14).

KING SAUL AND KING DAVID

The biblical depiction of king Saul and king David sheds light on what kings should and should not be. Christians today are not under the Old Covenant, so the point is not that modern civil authorities should operate precisely how a faithful Israelite king would have in the Old Testament. Moreover, the story of Saul and David has the ultimate purpose of foreshadowing the great rule and reign of our Lord Jesus Christ. However, there is still immense wisdom for civil government that can be obtained from an analysis of Saul's demise and David's rise to the throne.

Saul was a king like those that ruled other nations (1 Samuel 8:5). He was just the king Israel wanted. Israel wanted a king and could indeed have had a good king. The time of the judges, which preceded the monarchy, was not ideal—"In those days there was no king in Israel. Everyone did what was right in his own eyes" (Judges 21:25). Before they entered the Promised Land, God told Israel what their king must be like, "you may indeed set a king over you whom the LORD your God will choose" (Deuteronomy 17:15). God made clear that Israel's king must adhere to His Word:

> And when he sits on the throne of his kingdom, he shall write for himself in a book a copy of this law, approved by the Levitical priests. And it shall be with him, and he shall read in it all the days of his life, that he may learn to fear the LORD his God by keeping all the words of this law and these statutes, and doing them, that his heart may not be lifted up above his brothers, and that he may not turn aside from the commandment, either to the right hand or to the left, so that he may continue long in his kingdom, he and his children, in Israel (Deuteronomy 17:18-20).

Saul, however, routinely turned away from God's commandment, opting to abide by his own. He illustrates the problem with a large swath of American civil leaders.

Saul was often afraid. He feared Goliath. He feared the Philistines. He feared David. A nation gets into a lot of trouble when its leaders fear man rather than God. Fearing man, Saul tracked along an awful trajectory. He spiraled downward, learning to trust himself more and more, which was a terrible idea. He offered a sacrifice that he was not permitted to offer (1 Samuel 13:8). He made a rash vow, foolishly making his army fight without the strength that comes from food (1 Samuel 14:24). And he left God's war assignment unfulfilled, thinking it wiser to spare a wicked king whom God said was to die (1 Samuel 15:9).

As a godless king, Saul exalted himself. He was jealous of David. He could not handle when the ladies sang of David killing many more thousands than he had killed. He did not listen to wise counsel. His very own son Jonathan tried to turn him aside from destructive pursuits. Saul, like Pharaoh, initially said he would comply with wise counsel. But, shortly after that, he would go about his own way again. Doing so, Saul burdened his people. Israel suffered under the king like the nations. They lost in battle. And the many curses which God had warned them about came to pass. The prophet Samuel relayed God's message to Israel as they demanded a king like the nations:

> He will take your sons and appoint them to his chariots and to be his horsemen and to run before his chariots. And he will appoint for himself commanders of thousands and commanders of fifties, and some to plow his ground and to reap his harvest, and to make his implements of war and the equipment of his chariots. He will take your daughters to be perfumers and cooks and bakers. He will take the best of your fields and vineyards and olive orchards and give them to his servants. He will take the tenth of your grain and of your vineyards and give it to his officers and to his servants. He will take your male servants and female servants and the best of your young men and your donkeys, and put them to his work. He will take the tenth of your flocks, and you shall be his slaves (1 Samuel 8:11-17).

America currently experiences this very tyranny. We have demanded civil leaders who reject the King of Kings. We suffer the slavery of our decision.

It is remarkable that even in Saul's rebellion, he confirmed God's truthfulness and reign. Saul once pursued David to murder him, only to end up prostrate, naked, prophesying God's truth (1 Samuel 19:24). He found himself in a Nebedchudnezzar-like situation, cursed by the King of Kings for kingly malpractice. Even as he approached his death, Saul ended up a witness to the truthfulness of God. The Lord would not speak to Saul anymore. So Saul went to a medium, one who corresponded with the dead—a practice outlawed by God's Word and even Saul himself. Saul had proven to be a pragmatic king, untethered from God's revelation, so there was no problem with him transgressing both God's Word and his own. As he arrived at the medium's house, the message he received from a dead prophet resulted in Saul falling to the ground in great terror. The Word of God leveled the king to the ground.

So it will be in our day. However trampled on by our civil authorities, the Word of God will be the very thing that results in their downfall. His Word is true though every man were a liar. Christians need not fear that an American president or representative can somehow snuff out the Word of Christ. The snuffing out works in the other direction.

David was a king unlike Saul. He was a king after God's own heart. Yes, he made plenty of mistakes; he sinned in grievous ways. Yet he illustrates how kings are to fear God and follow His Word.

Saul was often afraid, but David was often courageous. He faced beasts as a shepherd and Goliath on the field of battle.

He could do so because he relied on God rather than himself. He believed what Saul doubted when he said to Goliath, "For the battle is the LORD's, and he will give you into our hand" (1 Samuel 17:47). His high view of God resulted in appropriate humility. He would not raise his hand against Saul, the Lord's anointed. When he had multiple opportunities to kill Saul, he refrained. When reasoning with Saul that he was no threat to him, David referred to himself as a dog and a flea (1 Samuel 24:14). In his humility, David listened to wise counsel. Abigail persuaded David away from the foolish pursuit of killing her husband, Nabal. And when David won a great battle against the Amalekites, he sent gifts to the elders and towns of Judah—"When David came to Ziklag, he sent part of the spoil to his friends, the elders of Judah, saying, 'Here is a present for you from the spoil of the enemies of the LORD'" (1 Samuel 30:26).

Saul was a taking king. David was a giving king. Saul was a prideful king. David was a humble king. Saul refused to listen. David heard out his counselors. Saul ignored God. David loved God. Saul disregarded God's Word. David sought out God's Word. Saul spiraled down to death at the hands of his enemies. David ascended to the throne, handing over that throne to his son at his death. If we would teach kings to observe all that Christ has commanded, we must exhort them to follow David, not Saul.

PRAY FOR CIVIL AUTHORITIES

Teaching kings includes praying for them. We have operated for far too long without God in our civil government. There will be no recovery of the fear of God among our civil leaders without revival. We cannot manufacture what needs to be done. The godless worldview that advances among us consists of identifying problems with the human eye and fixing them with the human hand. But the mind and aid of God do not enter into the equation. While Christians are all for identifying and fixing problems, we know that apart from Christ, we can do nothing (John 15:5). Our prayers themselves set us apart from the new religion. We are a people who humble ourselves and pray, knowing only God can heal.

The apostle Paul tells us explicitly in the New Testament that we are to pray for kings:

> First of all, then, I urge that supplications, prayers, intercessions, and thanksgivings be made for all people, for kings and all who are in high positions, that we may lead a peaceful and quiet life, godly and dignified in every way. This is good, and it is pleasing in the sight of God our Savior, who desires all people to be saved and to come to the knowledge of the truth. For there is one God, and there is one mediator between God and men, the man Christ Jesus, who gave himself as a ransom for all, which is the testimony given at the proper time (1 Timothy 2:1-6).

Those who regularly engage in the political realm must be diligent in prayer. Given the secular humanism of our times, there will be great temptation—"bad company corrupts good morals" (1 Corinthians 15:33). But prayer for kings is not only the responsibility of the politically engaged. Families ought to seek the welfare of their civil authorities through prayer in the home. Our sons and daughters, grandsons and granddaughters, ought to grow up in homes where civil leaders are named before the throne of grace. Likewise, church worship includes intercession for civil magistrates. In our worship services at Grace Baptist Church, we pray weekly for civil leaders, no matter their party or positions. Indeed, our intercessions will take different shapes depending on the civil leader's character and actions, but intercession is commanded by God for our civil leaders no matter who they are.

HONOR AND SUBMIT TO CIVIL AUTHORITIES

We must teach kings through honoring and submitting to them. The apostle Peter instructs,

> Be subject for the Lord's sake to every human institution, whether it be to the emperor as supreme, or to governors as sent by him to punish those who do evil and to praise those who do good. For this is the will of God, that by doing good you should put to silence the ignorance of foolish people. Live as people who are free, not using your freedom as a cover-up for evil, but living as servants of God. Honor everyone. Love the brotherhood. Fear God. Honor the emperor (1 Peter 2:13-17).

Christians teach the truth about God by not chafing under authority. It is the spirit of the new religion that cannot handle having a boss or a law. We are happy to have civil leaders, knowing that Christ has established them in their positions for our good.

Everyone feels the difficulty of determining how to honor civil authorities who operate in dishonorable ways. We will not make the right determination if we neglect the truth that civil kings serve under Jesus. We do not honor human authorities by dishonoring divine authority. When civil magistrates do dishonorable things publicly, it is no transgression of Peter's instruction to address those shameful things publicly. You can certainly address the sin of civil magistrates in a dishonorable way. We do not commend doing so. But to lovingly speak the truth about an authority's sin is not to dishonor that authority.

When President Trump tweeted that it was his "great honor" to be recognized as "the most pro-gay President in American history," Tom responded directly to him in the President's domain of choice by tweeting back, "While all people should be treated with respect as image-bearers of God, being 'pro-gay' or 'pro-LGBTQ' is no honor Mr. President. It is shameful & unloving to the very people you think you are supporting. You are God's servant. Please repent."[1] This was an attempt to remind him, as well as others, that he, too, is under the authority of Jesus Christ.

PREACH TO CIVIL AUTHORITIES

We see this very kind of truth-telling in Psalm 2. The psalmist says, "Now therefore, O kings, be wise; be warned, O rulers of the earth. Serve the LORD with fear, and rejoice with trembling. Kiss the Son, lest he be angry, and you perish in the way, for his wrath is quickly kindled. Blessed are all who take refuge in him" (Psalm 2:10-12). We have here a model for preaching to civil authorities.

As we preach to civil leaders, we must first address them as fallen image-bearers. Every civil leader is a creature created in the image of God. Like every other person, he has sinned and needs the redemption which God supplies through His Son. You cannot get Christian fruit without the Christian root. Indeed, certain unbelieving kings have a God-given ability to lead in better ways than others. We find leaders

---

1 Tom Ascol, Twitter post, August 21, 2020, 9:22 a.m., https://twitter. com/tomascol/status/1296799823190990848.

who, while dead in their sins, can still be spoken of as gifted with a measure of natural understanding and ability to influence others in helpful ways. Even so, as we saw with Saul and David above, you will not be able to get the fear of God in our kingly rule if the heart of the king is spiritually dead.

As we preach the saving message to kings, we also must disciple them. We are not permitted to stop at, "Trust in the Lord and be saved." If we stop at that point, then we will not fulfill the very commandment Jesus has given us. He told us to teach people of all nations to observe all he has commanded (Matthew 28:20). Civil authorities are not exempt from pastoral care, instruction, and discipleship.

This point is far more significant than many think. American culture has left civil leaders without discipleship. When is the last time you heard of a civil leader being excommunicated from a church? It almost never happens. But, we claim to have halls full of Christian leaders, many of whom have done things worthy of church discipline. Civil leaders feel that they cannot afford accountability of that nature. And the church has no desire to hold them accountable in that way. We have put civil authorities in a special class, one in which the common expectations of church attendance, membership, and discipleship are non-existent.

Kings must be taught how to follow Jesus. Discipleship must include the bread and butter of repentance and faith that marks any Christian's life. They must read the Scripture, pray, worship God with the church, and fulfill family obligations and commitments. But every Christian must learn how Jesus would have them work, given their station in life. Husbands, for example, are to love their wives. Wives are to respect their husbands. Elders are to shepherd the flock of God that is among them (1 Peter 5:2). The rich are not to be haughty, nor to set their hopes on the uncertainty of riches, but on God, who richly provides us with everything to enjoy (1 Timothy 6:17). When any individual is discipled, his or her particular station is not off-limits from Christ's instruction.

Civil authorities, then, must be taught what Christ would have them do as civil authorities. Christians must teach civil magistrates what it means that they are God's ministers. We have fallen terribly short in this duty. For example, what would a modern judge say if you asked him, "Do you think of yourself as one who carries out God's wrath on the wrong-doer?" Many of the judges across our land have no sense of that central definition of their job description (Romans 13:4). The same goes for legislators. While they are not, like judges, tasked with the specific work of bringing down the sword, they do determine through legislation the crimes which will be punished by the sword. In that sense, they carry out God's wrath. How can our civil leaders do what Jesus has commanded them to do as civil leaders if Christians have failed to teach them the very nature of their position?

Believers must also teach civil authorities how to fulfill their God-defined position. We do not mean that any Christian can educate a civil authority on the intricacies of modern political work. But Christians, in general, are to teach the basic principles involved in ruling well in the fear of God. Legislators need to learn God's law so that they will know how to make good laws. Governors need to consider the Great Governor's character and work so that they will lead with wisdom. Judges must know God's law and His gospel so that they would render down just decisions. Civil authorities must do their work by faith. If it is done without faith, then in an ultimate sense, it will not be done as God designed.

MODEL AND LEAD IN THE CIVIL REALM

Given the godlessness of our times, our civil leaders will need models. Christians must teach them by modeling civil leadership and the happy assumption of responsibility for neighbor and nation. Christians must become much more involved in city council meetings, county assemblies, and the state of their society in general. We must educate ourselves on the wisdom that Scripture provides regarding civil life and how our particular cities, counties, states, and nation match up to that picture. Work is required if we are to take responsibility in these ways. We have heard stories of civil officials simply not hearing from Christians. They hear from people with other agendas. And those voices shape how civil leaders rule.

Regrettably, Christians have failed to engage civilly, in part because of a faulty doctrinal understanding. We have retracted from political engagement, often due to despair. As the new religion rises, there is great temptation to pull back even further. Some may think that we simply need to labor in our churches and go underground. Of course, we need to labor in our churches. And hardship—maybe even regular persecution—appears to be on the horizon. But, more than ever, we need Christians who are unashamed to live publicly for Christ. We need pastors ready to go to prison if church bans remain or increase. We need Christians bearing witness in city meetings to what God has said about abortion. We need open conversations, full of grace and truth and seasoned with salt, about the best city, county, state, and national policies on a whole host of issues.

THINGS NOT DONE IN A CORNER

In the Bible, those who followed God were always getting in trouble in the civil realm. They were not merely losing civil influence and freedoms while quietly accepting it, which is sadly the case in America quite often. The Canaanite kings objected to Israelite faithfulness to the Lord. Pharaoh and the Egyptians came into conflict with Israel's obedience to God. The Jewish leadership could not abide Christ and His followers. The Romans could not sit idly by and watch Jesus and His followers turn the world upside down. In every city, the public felt the force of the gospel of Jesus Christ.

We must resolve to bear witness to Christ, His gospel, and His kingdom. As we do, we will join with our forefathers in seeing the glorious impact of God's Word in our civil life. We are not guaranteed exactly what that impact will look like. But, we are guaranteed that it will be glorious. May our voice resound with the wonder of the apostle Paul's as he stood before kings to testify to God's truth:

> "To this day I have had the help that comes from God, and so I stand here testifying both to small and great, saying nothing but what the prophets and Moses said would come to pass: that the Christ must suffer and that, by being the first to rise from the dead, he would proclaim light both to our people and to the Gentiles."

And as he was saying these things in his defense, Festus said with a loud voice, "Paul, you are out of your mind; your great learning is driving you out of your mind." But Paul said, "I am not out of my mind, most excellent Festus, but I am speaking true and rational words. For the king knows about these things, and to him I speak boldly. For I am persuaded that none of these things has escaped his notice, for this has not been done in a corner" (Acts 26:22-26).

Conclusion

BE STRONG AND COURAGEOUS: FOLLOWING JESUS WITH JOY

America is anything but a united nation under God. At the founding of our country, there was an undeniable Christian influence at the root of our civil life. Over many years, we have polluted that Christian soil, steadily sewing it with ideas contrary to Christ. A religious impulse inspires the unraveling of our nation. Many Christians are trying to decide where to stand. The prophet Elijah has a word for us, "How long will you go limping between two different opinions? If the LORD is God, follow him; but if Baal, then follow him" (1 Kings 18:21). Until you see it in those terms, you will not be able to operate Christianly.

Jesus has told us to deny ourselves, take up our cross, and follow Him (Luke 9:23). Doing so has always been costly and lovely. It has always involved public witness and sacrifice. We are not permitted to say that we are with Jesus while neglecting to follow Him before the eyes of a watching world. We contend that the church's widespread unwillingness to follow Jesus publicly has, in part, brought about our nation's trouble. Christians cannot point the finger and shirk responsibility for the rise of America's new religion. We must instead repent of our complicity and, in humble dependence on God, announce Christ's gospel to lost sinners while adorning that gospel with our lives.

THE NEW RELIGION

Perhaps the clearest way to articulate America's new religion is to see that we have turned to worship the creature rather than the Creator. Man, the creature, is now god. But in our current situation, it is not exactly the individual man who is god. Rather, collectivist man is god. We are all in this god thing together. And you will come along, or else. So, everyone must bow down to the whole society of men and women. Granted, all sorts of deceivers do not really practice this new religion. They merely play the "we are all god" game to get whatever they can—"their god is their belly" (Philippians 3:19).

Nevertheless, they must pretend to practice it. And if we are all god together, what then needs to happen? Well, there must be universal equality and uniformity that occurs among all peoples. Collectivist man, being god, cannot be divided. One may not be different than another. No harmony permitted. One may not have more or less than another. Such a reality is not only an injustice in the new religion. It is blasphemous. We have not yet attained this glorious utopia, but one day, male, female, black, white, heterosexual, homosexual, (insert your intersectional category of choice) will all have exactly the same belongings. If we just believe in ourselves, then all will come to pass. Why would we not believe in ourselves? We are god, after all.

In our city, a mural with a new take on the Lord's Supper was recently commissioned. In place of the apostles, it pictures various outcasts including a transgender individual, a cross-dressing alcoholic, a little black girl, and a Middle Eastern mother with her child. A white mega-church pastor plays the part of Judas, who has gotten up to leave the table. Jesus Himself is portrayed as "a vagabond black man, showing how much value is hidden within those from whom many may expect little."[1] While Jesus indeed gathers to Himself the broken and the needy, it is not hard to see that this mural portrays much more. It is a depiction of America's new religion. You have the Lord's Supper with no Lord Jesus. He has been replaced with a mere human in whom we must see great value. The bread and cup of the Lord's Supper, which symbolize Christ's body and blood for our salvation, has been replaced with a cheeseburger and soda, the former being offered to a street dog and the latter to a homeless woman.

America's new faith manifests itself in many ways. In the unrest of 2020, white people and police officers washed the feet of black leaders, asking for forgiveness.[2] In another case, a Black Lives Matter representative, who was white, approached a white woman on the street, telling her to kneel and apologize for her whiteness. She did so, working hard to make sure she gave an honest and accurate confession. During the 2020 riots, instructions were given to mark your entrance with "minority-owned" to protect your store from looting. These instructions are eerily similar to the Lord's instructions to Israel during Passover. Mark your door with blood, and the angel of death will pass over. When the media announced that Joe Biden had won the 2020 presidential

---

1 Ross Boone, "Modern Last Supper," Raw Spoon, accessed November 25, 2020, https://www.rawspoon.com/last-supper-art.

2 Peter Heck, "White citizens and police officers wash feet of black leaders, ask for forgiveness," Disrn, June 9, 2020, https://disrn.com/news/white-citizens-and-police-officers-wash-feet-of-black-leaders-ask-for-forgiveness.

election, California governor Gavin Newsom shared on social media, "Spread the faith."[3]

HAVE I NOT COMMANDED YOU?

The new religion is nothing to fear. God is worthy of our reverence and fear, but not the hardened secularism that manifests itself in the immature civil leadership, social interactions, and art mentioned above.

We do not mean, however, that following Jesus amid the increase of our nation's worldliness will be easy. We regularly hear from Christians who suffer ridicule, shame, loss of employment, and many other challenges due to the spirit of the age. If the trajectory holds, then more trouble will come. When Jesus sent His twelve disciples out, He told them, "Behold, I am sending you out as sheep in the midst of wolves." Why did He choose that imagery? Sheep have no resources in themselves to provide protection from wolves. Wolves prey on sheep to devour them. If sheep are to survive—even more so, if they are to thrive and positively impact wolves—it will be by power from beyond themselves. That is precisely what Jesus wants us to understand as we think of our engagement in the world. It is also why He adds this admonition to that description of our situation: "so be wise as serpents and innocent as doves" (Matthew 10:16). Modern American Christians seem to have the dove part down pretty well. In this book, we have tried to encourage embracing the shrewdness of serpents that our Lord also commands.

Jesus tells us, "In the world you will have tribulation. But take heart; I have overcome the world" (John 16:33).

---

3 Gavin Newsom, Twitter Post, November 7, 2020, 8:55 p.m., https://twitter.com/GavinNewsom/status/1325255673349693440?s=20.

Christians have a rich, two-thousand-year heritage of joyfully living for God in His world. Jesus redeemed us, and in so doing, testified the truth of God before a hostile world. We have the remarkable privilege of joining Him in that testimony. He went about His work joyfully. How could we do any different?

This book has laid out a vision for following Jesus as American culture and civil society externalize more and more of its inner and erroneous faith commitment. We have identified the general nature of America's new religion as the creature-worship spoken of by the apostle Paul in Romans 1. It maintains a false hope, which must be rejected, fueled by a spirit of anarchy and advanced by tyrannical government. Christians must go on the offense, refusing to run and hide from the situation in which we find ourselves. That advance includes taking responsibility to address our social confusion and lawlessness, ruling well as citizen kings, embracing the freedom of slavery to Christ, and facing up to the danger. We must follow Jesus in these ways not only as individuals, but in our homes, churches, and civil life.

It may feel that you are surrounded on every side by trouble. That is a perfectly fine position for believers in the Almighty to be. Israel was once in that condition. We would do well to adopt the spirit of Joab:

> When Joab saw that the battle was set against him both in front and in the rear, he chose some of the best men of Israel and arrayed them against the Syrians. The rest of his men he put in the charge of Abishai his brother, and he arrayed them against the Ammonites. And he said, "If the Syrians are too strong for me, then you shall help me, but if the Ammonites are too strong for you, then I will come

and help you. Be of good courage, and let us be courageous for our people, and for the cities of our God, and may the LORD do what seems good to him" (2 Samuel 10:9-12).

One thing is certain. We are not free to back away from following Jesus. Jesus is the son of God who became man for us and for our salvation. He was born of the virgin Mary and suffered under Pontius Pilate. He died on the cross in our place for our sins. And He has risen to life, never to die again. Through faith in Him, we have been forgiven. At bottom, America has nothing we want, and we have nothing she can take. We are the blood-bought children of God, called to proclaim the excellencies of Him who called us out of darkness into His marvelous light (1 Peter 2:9). We will not go do Christ's work in a corner because of America's new religion. Jesus advances His truth throughout the world, and we will follow Him.

Be strong and courageous, for you shall cause this people to inherit the land that I swore to their fathers to give them. Only be strong and very courageous, being careful to do according to all the law that Moses my servant commanded you. Do not turn from it to the right hand or to the left, that you may have good success wherever you go. This Book of the Law shall not depart from your mouth, but you shall meditate on it day and night, so that you may be careful to do according to all that is written in it. For then you will make your way prosperous, and then you will have good success. Have I not commanded you? Be strong and courageous. Do not be frightened, and do not be dismayed, for the LORD your God is with you wherever you go" (Joshua 1:6-9).

Appendix 1

GOD'S WORD IN GODLESS TIMES

Tom Ascol

But understand this, that in the last days there will come times of difficulty. For people will be lovers of self, lovers of money, proud, arrogant, abusive, disobedient to their parents, ungrateful, unholy, heartless, unappeasable, slanderous, without self-control, brutal, not loving good, treacherous, reckless, swollen with conceit, lovers of pleasure rather than lovers of God, having the appearance of godliness, but denying its power. Avoid such people. For among them are those who creep into households and capture weak women, burdened with sins and led astray by various passions, always learning and never able to arrive at a knowledge of the truth (2 Timothy 3:1-7).

Read those seven verses of God's words again. Slowly. Now go check your twitter feed or simply do a social media search for #GeorgeFloyd, #GeorgeFloydProtests, and #GeorgeFloydRiots. Paul is talking about America in 2020. Just as he was talking about Ephesus in the late AD 60s as well as about other times and places between then and now. He is speaking of recurring "times of difficulty"—perilous times; what he elsewhere describes as "the evil day" (Ephesians 6:13).

Such seasons will be characterized by severe problems in society as "people" (v. 2) in general will give themselves over to the types of wickedness Paul catalogues in verses 2-4. Such wickedness is characterized by selfishness ("lovers of self, lovers of money, proud, arrogant") and lawlessness ("abusive, disobedient to their parents, ungrateful, unholy, heartless, unappeasable, slanderous, without self-control, brutal, not loving good, treacherous, reckless, swollen with conceit, lovers of pleasure rather than lovers of God").

That is bad enough. What is worse, however, is that godlessness in society does not stay there but seeps into the church wreaking havoc among the people of God. The most unsettling part of what Paul says is coming is his description of how professing Christians will act. They will be "having the appearance of godliness, but denying its power" (v. 5).

Paul further describes these people within the church in verse 7—they will be unteachable, "always learning and never able to arrive at a knowledge of the truth." Even more to the point, he warns in chapter 4, "For the time is coming when people will not endure sound teaching, but having itching ears they will accumulate for themselves teachers to suit their own passions and will turn away from listening to the truth" and will "wander off into myths" (vv. 3-4).

I am convinced that America is living in a peculiarly "evil day," in "times of difficulty" of which Paul writes. The outbreak of lawlessness in our nation is evil. Mayhem, brutal attacks, destruction of people's livelihood, intimidation, violence, and murder have marked the protests of 2020.

Attacks on police officers, breaking into private homes, looting, stealing, and blatantly breaking just laws have become almost commonplace.

True godliness unashamedly declares what God has said and it does so not just when it is safe but even when that message might cost your life.

Such lawlessness in our society is tragic. But what is worse is the failure and even complicity of so many Christians in the face of it. In their responses they have, as Paul puts it, an appearance of godliness that denies its power (v. 3:5). True godliness unashamedly declares what God has said and it does so not just when it is safe but even when that message might cost your life. It is taking God at His Word regardless of cost or consequence and speaking that Word with confidence in its power. Thus, John the Baptist didn't merely preach repentance in the wilderness, he also applied God's Word to Herod that by telling him that he could not lawfully have his brother's wife (Matthew 14:1-12).

The mere "appearance of godliness," by contrast, is willing to say what God says only when it isn't costly. If doing so actually elevates you in the eyes of the curators of the prevailing cultural narrative, then more's the better. It is what today is commonly called, virtue signaling. That is what a person does when he would rather be perceived as virtuous and applauded by the modern arbiters of "virtue" than actually be virtuous and risk being canceled as a result.

It's sort of like the German *Landeskirchen* preaching on submission to governmental authorities in Nazi Germany. No one got arrested for that. But it was a failure of nerve, or rather, a denying of the power of godliness, that kept most German Protestants from speaking against the anti-Semitic butchery in 1941. It is easy to go with religion when she walks in silver slippers.

The prevalence of an apparent but impotent godliness is being widely and prominently paraded today. That is why you have seen such bold, articulate outcries against the lawlessness of Derek Chauvin but only reluctant, comparatively muted responses to the lawlessness of the violent mobs that have terrorized cities and communities across the nation in the days since. That is why demands for justice are readily applied to the former but only hesitantly—if at all—to the latter. That is why you saw so many evangelicals following the crowd in #BlackoutTuesday on their social media feeds, some even sporting the Black Lives Matter (BLM) hashtag for extra virtue points. Never mind that the BLM organization and movement intentionally promote godlessness in their stated goals and focus.

That is why you know the names of Breonna Taylor, Ahmaud Arbery, and George Floyd but not the names of David Dorn, Italia Kelly, and others. From all indications they unjustly suffered violent deaths but only the first three serve the destructive agendas of those who want to rip apart the fabric of our civil society. True godliness is willing to apply the standard of God's Word to every case. Apparent godliness will stop at the first three because to speak further is to invite the vitriol of the mob and, well, who has the power to withstand that?

So, what are Christians who fear God more than people to do in such godless, evil days? We are to do exactly what Paul tells Timothy to do in 2 Timothy 3:14-15 and 4:1-5. First, continue in the Word, and second, preach the Word.

It is the Holy Scripture that God breathed out to be our authoritative, sufficient guide for life and godliness. It alone is "profitable for teaching, for reproof, for correction, and for training in righteousness, that the man of God may be competent, equipped for every good work" (vv. 3:16-17). Such a man—especially pastors—must, like Timothy, preach that Word at all times with authority and conviction. That is what Paul means when he writes, "preach the word; be ready in season and out of season; reprove, rebuke, and exhort, with complete patience and teaching" (v. 4:2).

This is to be done even when people don't want to hear it; when they "will not endure sound teaching" (v. 4:3) and "turn away from listening to the truth and wander off into myths" (v. 4:4). The Word alone is able to make people "wise for salvation through faith in Christ Jesus" (v. 3:15). So, if we who know the Lord and have His Word fail to preach it, we are withholding the only message that God has provided to reconcile sinners to Himself. And all the virtue signaling in the world cannot change that.

So this is the choice that Christians are facing in times of difficulty. We can settle for an appearance of godliness while denying its power and win the accolades of this age. Or we can pursue real godliness and trust its power thereby inviting the venom and opposition of the champions of this age. To put it another way, we can signal false virtue and be welcomed by those operating on false principles of righteousness. Or we can practice genuine virtue and be welcomed by the God whose Word we refuse to compromise.

What we cannot do is have it both ways.

Appendix 2

PAGAN AMERICA DRESSED IN CHRISTIANITY

Jared Longshore

The events which unfolded in America in the year 2020 have been tragic. Civil unrest spread across the nation with the tragic killing of George Floyd by a Minneapolis police officer. Rather than grieve and seek true justice, many have gone to set America on fire. We need to make sense of things from a Christian perspective.

The apostle Paul adds an unexpected phrase in one of his letters to Timothy. After speaking of the coming perilous times, and the rampant wickedness of men in those times, he says people will have "a form of godliness" but deny its power (2 Timothy 3:5). This "form of godliness," gutted of substance, is precisely what is going on around us. And nearly everybody is guilty. We are watching the erosion of the Christian faith while everyone masquerades as Christian.

This is not, however, the first time such a thing has occurred. You can see the draining of Christian substance while maintaining *a form of it* in a string of paintings from the 15th century.[1] In 1435, Van Eyck painted the *Madonna of the Chancellor Rolin*, in which Chancellor Rolin sits facing Mary. Mary looks about how you would expect she should. She has both the form of Mary and the substance of Mary. But, in Filippo Lippi's painting of Mary some years later, he made a change—he painted *his mistress* as Mary. In Lippi's painting you have the form of Mary, but in substance, a scandal. Things unravel further with Fouquet's painting of Mary in c.1450 (Virgin and Child). He paints the king's mistress, Agnes Sorel, as Mary. He paints her with one breast exposed (not feeding the Christ-child). The painting speaks for itself (I leave it to your discretion whether to look it up). It has moved far afield from Van Eyck and Lippi. Even secular analysis has marked it as impious with a flavor of blasphemy. The *form* barely remains; the Christian substance is dead.

America is Fouquet's 1450 *Virgin and Child*. We have reached the end of the line. The substance is gone, but a number of people are still holding on to *the form* of Christianity. While doing so, they are trying to convert others to their paganism dressed in Christianity. But if the substance is gone, then anyone converted will join a false religion impersonating the true religion. Many evangelicals are busy trying to reconcile this false religion with the true Christian faith. But they cannot be reconciled. Others, perhaps who do not grasp exactly what is going on, try to harmonize the two. They labor for common ground with the spirit of the age. But there is no common ground. There is no harmony.

---

1 For an analysis of these paintings see Francis Schaeffer, *Escape from Reason* (Downers Grove, IL: InterVarsity Press, 1968), 20-22.

THE RIOTERS

The rioters who filled the streets of the United States engaged in violence and anarchy. But they claimed a form of godliness. There indeed were many peaceful protestors. Some have displayed courage by shutting down rioters. But the rioters themselves are a different story. They justify their lawlessness by saying they have not been heard. Their actions are righteous, reasonable, and what other people need to do is sit down and listen. If you are on the side of the oppressed (like Jesus), then you must be on their side. If you desire the sanctification of our nation, then put on your mask and throw that brick through a window. Let your voice be heard. Black lives matter, don't they? What we are observing is not merely a group of misguided adolescents. We are observing rebellion driven by a religious impulse. The rioters are crying out to their governmental gods much like the false prophets cried out to Baal to send fire. They claim to have a holy mission. But there is only a shell of godliness here, no power.

EVANGELICAL RESPONSE

The evangelical response to our troubled times has been elegantly vacuous. Christian leaders have justified lawless riots. Many have promoted organizations that advocate wickedness. A number of evangelicals and churches participated in blackout Tuesday without knowing what it was. While there are some who have addressed our times with conviction, many evangelical leaders appear to be posturing without getting down to the real issue. A common term for what we are seeing many evangelicals do is virtue signaling. But consider what that term describes. Evangelicals signal that they are virtuous while in reality being the opposite. They claim to seek justice and equality while in truth they pursue the praise of man. Like Fouquet's painting, evangelicals signal religion, but we are neglecting the substance and power.

How Did We Get Here?

Schaffer once said that if the lower story becomes untethered from the upper story, then the lower story devours the upper story. This is precisely what is happening. And Christians have to take responsibility for their part in letting things get here. Jesus came *in the flesh*. If you teach that he didn't, then the apostle John says you are antichrist (1 John 4:3). But we have lived for some time as if Jesus is just *an idea* and Christianity has nothing to do with life on earth. We have lived as if Christianity were contained to the upper world, having nothing at all to do with the lower world. We have mistaken Hebrews, which says faith is the "conviction of things unseen," to say that faith is the conviction of things *unknown*—as if our faith were imaginary. In other words, we have given into a radical, unbridgeable divide between the sacred and the secular. Rather than mere Christians, we have become mere pragmatists... except on Sundays and at our Bible studies.

Black Lives Matter is a pragmatic movement. Many of our political leaders are given to pragmatism. And evangelicals are the lead pragmatists of them all. We have lived in the lower world without God. He has had nothing to do with our vocation, entertainment, politics, sex, art, economics, civil law, customs, and cultural traditions. God is God of our quiet times, but there His jurisdiction stops. We enjoy the freedom of worship within the four walls of our church but have no concept of the full exercise of religion at all times and in all places. We support an educational institution that has told us plainly that God is not welcome. The Christian faith has been relegated to the upper world for a very long time now, leaving secular humanism to rule in the lower world. That lower philosophy is devouring that upper faith (which we should have never lodged up there in the first place).

Ironically, we are watching the erosion of that Christian faith while politicians, rioters, and evangelical leaders *claim* they are protecting and promoting that Christian faith. They can get away with this because we have permitted the notion that Christianity is not real but a dream. If a dream, then Jesus can become whatever you want him to be. There is merely an outline of him in the American psyche, and people fill that outline with whatever they want, like Fouquet filled Mary's form with the king's mistress, Agnes Sorel.

We must avoid, then, the mindset which says, "Lay down your ideology and presuppositions, and just give people Jesus." Those who recommend this are either trying to smuggle an unbiblical ideology into the Christian church, or being duped into letting others do so. Those who recommend this will end up offering the form of Jesus without the substance. Schaffer once said,

> I have come to the point where, when I hear the word 'Jesus'—which means so much to me because of the Person of the historic Jesus and his work, I listen carefully because I have with sorrow become more afraid of the word 'Jesus' than almost any other word in the modern world. The word is used as a contentless banner, and our generation is invited to follow it... we must fight this contentless banner, with its deep motivations... which is being used for the purpose of sociological form and control.[2]

---

2 Ibid., 100.

THE WAY FORWARD

The first thing to do is acknowledge that much of what presently purports to be Christianity is merely Fouquet's *Virgin and Child*—an empty shell. It is Jesus without the Christian faith. It is a naked adulteress posing as the mother of God. It is high time we come to grips with the vanity of such Christianity lest we end up caught in it like Samson who "did not know that the Lord had left him" (Judges 16:20).

The next thing we must do is deal with the God *who is here*. He is the Word made flesh. He speaks. He is handing America over to her sins. He is King up there and down here. He is a Savior-King who willingly laid down His life for those who cast off His law and have done what was right in their own eyes. In short, we must fear God. To know Him savingly is to know Him soul and body. To know Him truly is to know Him in heaven and on earth. To come to Him, you must come away from everything else. You cannot fit a Christless ideology into Christ. You cannot fit Christless living into the Christian life. You cannot sanitize evil notions of justice, power, authority, reconciliation, mercy, and love, and make them Christian. You must come wholly away from all of that to the whole Christ.

Scripture Index

Old Testament

New Testament